Dear Boo
Volunteering has endless
challenges and great
satisfaction - Hope you
enjoy the gift from your Mom

All our Best

Annette and Goldye

-1   7k
         2|2
         8||

ANNETTE SHAPIRO

ANNETTE SHAPIRO

PROFESSIONAL VOLUNTEER

BY GOLDYE HARRIS

Rose Press
Beverly Hills

Published by Rose Press
P.O. Box 17115
Beverly Hills, CA 90291

Printed in the United States of America – 1994
Book design by David Goodnick
First edition

To our grandchildren: The future

Erin, Ben, Stephen, Natalie and William Shapiro
Jordan and Courtney Teller
Annette Shapiro

Jacob Maurice Harris and Deborah Harris
Goldye Harris

About Annette Shapiro and This Book

𝒥n a given span of time, unique personalities are rare. Annette Shapiro is one of those rare, unique personalities. Her extraordinary work as "professional volunteer"(her own proudly self-designated title) during the past four decades in the jewish and general communites has enriched her and our world. She has truly made a difference.

Volunteerism in our society has changed over the years, some of its old passion having diminished somewhat. Yet our community cannot exist without the volunteer. The initiative, time and expertise of our lay leaders are crucial and absolutely essential if the American and Jewish enterprises are to be healing and are to flourish. And I would add – the volunteer working for a cause larger than and beyond oneself is one of the surest paths to that volunteer's personal fulfillment.

Annette Shapiro embodies in her own life and work the finest objectives of volunteerism and the rich benefits such activity engenders. Such a life's work demanded chronicles for a larger audience as inspiration and guide for others. Here's this book, written in the hope of helping to bring about a rebirth of volunteerism in our needy contemporary society.

Heartfelt thanks to you, Annette, for enriching the lives of so many who have benefitted from (and through this book will continue to benefit from) the warm embrace of your open arms.

Dr. Jack Shechter
Dean of Continuing Education
University of Judaism

CONTENTS

WORDS FROM ANNETTE
ix

PREFACE
xiii

ONE
WHAT IS A PROFESSIONAL VOLUNTEER?
1

TWO
THE FAMILY
4

THREE
VOLUNTEERISM: THE BASIC ELEMENTS
16

FOUR
WHAT IS A LEADER?
22

FIVE
WHAT IS A WINNER?
30

SIX
GOOD JUDGEMENT
38

SEVEN
THE BOARD MEMBER
43

EIGHT
THE FINE ART OF NEGOTIATION
51

NINE
CONNECTIONS
56

CONTENTS

TEN
GETTING IT ALL TOGETHER
66

ELEVEN
MONEY
72

TWELVE
POWER
79

THIRTEEN
MILESTONES
85

FOURTEEN
THANK YOU
95

FIFTEEN
WHO AM I?
102

SIXTEEN
CONTINUANCE – CHANGES – CHOICES
108

EPILOGUE
113

A VOLUNTEER'S BIOGRAPHY
114

RECOGNITION & AWARDS
120

WORDS FROM ANNETTE

$\mathcal{J}$ hope this book will influence, direct and teach the value of volunteerism. If it helps to find a way to use your own talents and energies as a volunteer, then it will have been a worthwhile effort.

Volunteering offers individuals something we rarely find in the most prestigious and well-paying jobs: freedom, flexibility, and a chance to do work of your choice. My choice to be a professional volunteer is one that gives me the opportunity to grow and share my life with very special people. Being a volunteer gives you the chance to help in building a better world. I have found that causes devoted to improving the lot of individuals and the larger society are very important. It is just a matter of finding out for yourself where you fit and where you feel the most fulfillment.

The example of service to the community is a proud heritage given to me by my father, the late George Familian, and my mother, Rosella Familian Barbas. Growing up in the San Fernando Valley with my brother Arnold, and living next door to my father's brother, Isadore and his late wife, Sunny, and our cousins, Sandy Smalley and Gary Familian, gave us the opportunity to witness the Valley's growth while sharing our lives with the community and the Jewish people.

I have been fortunate, too, that my husband, Leonard, has inspired me to grow as an individual. His encouragement and understanding of my work in service to the community, which was influenced by his parents, Bertha and Fred Shapiro, of blessed memory, have been a source of support, but also a positive challenge.

Each member of my family has shared so much of my life and the activities I have been involved in. I feel that it is from them that I have learned the importance of family unity.

I want to extend my deepest thanks –

To my children:

David and his wife, Lynn; Joel; Ilyse (Lisi) and her husband, Steve Teller – and to my grandchildren – Erin, Ben, Stephen, Natalie, William, Jordan and Courtney.

To my extended family:

- Edith and Arnold Familian, their children, David Familian and his wife, Karen; Karen and her husband, Cliff Joyce; Bruce Familian and his wife, Arlene, and their grandchildren, Max, Ashley, Chelsea and Alex.

- My brother-in-law and sister-in-law, Bernard and Rena Shapiro and their children Susie and her husband Jaime Gesundheit; Linda Manasu; Alan Shapiro and his wife, Leslie; Gayle and her husband, David Egbert, and their grandchildren, Avi, Daniela, Michael, Kimberly, Brooke, Brian, Blake, Rebecca, Frederic and Sherwood.

- My brother-in-law and sister-in-law Herb and Mitzi Salkin; and to Betty Salkin, of blessed memory; her daughter, Maron, and her husband, Fred Holtz; and their grandchildren, Sara and Beverly.

To all my cousins who are many:

To them, and to all who read this book, I say that I am proud to pass along a heritage that offers so much fulfillment. You will discover, as I did, that the opportunity to share yourself with others is the worthiest inheritance.

Whatever opportunity you choose, whatever future you seek to fashion for yourself, believe in it, serve it and strive mightily to bring its rich rewards from dream to reality..

Acknowledgements

This book would not have been undertaken had it not been for the generous friendship of **Goldye Harris**. How does one acknowledge a friend and collaborator such as Goldye? We have shared years of involvement — me, as a volunteer, Goldye as the Campaign Director of the San Fernando Valley United Jewish Fund of Los Angeles, a professional, teacher and journalist. She has given me the opportunity and direction to develop, create and succeed in my choice of this profession.

Upon her retirement, she approached me with the idea of this book. In the pages that follow, Goldye and I have set down some recollections of my life and growth as a volunteer. She has managed, through many conversations, to take my thoughts and experiences and make them into a cohesive manuscript that reflects my career.

I am particularly thankful to **Rabbi Jack Shechter**, Dean of Continuing Education at the University of Judaism, consultant and empathetic friend, for his enthusiasm and editorial assistance, who made the various steps toward publication a pleasure. His conviction that this book is a worthwhile and important contribution to the role of a professional volunteer helped me to realize that the volume had to be written and gave me the fortitude to continue by providing me with encouragement at every step of the journey.

Alexis Joseph, my personal secretary and friend, who can hear my thoughts, has earned my genuine gratitude. My words flow from the computer as she calmly touches the keys with ease as I share my feelings. I thank her for the understanding and patience she has shown me over the years as I move from one project to another. Her presence in my life has enabled me to pursue a wide array of endeavors while she keeps my life in order.

I would also like to thank each of you – members of my family and friends – who have expressed your feelings about me in this book. The reflections of our relationship that you have shared here are very meaningful to me. If I have been able to add something to your lives, I am grateful. The confidence and support that each of you has expressed together with others whose lives I have touched, has given me the encouragement to pursue my career.

The writing of this book in partnership with everyone I have mentioned above has been another profound learning experience for me and has given me the opportunity for new growth. For that alone I am deeply grateful.

Annette Shapiro
Beverly Hills, California

PREFACE

Through the years working with volunteers as a professional in social work, and in self-help agencies as a journalist, public information director, publicist, and fundraiser, I had dreamed about writing a book. In the early years, I considered a torrid novel, fantasy fiction, imponderable mystery, self-help, "how-to," and so many other possibilities that came through my mind at various intervals of my life.

It was not until I retired, however, that the real incentive and available time became a reality. And then it occurred to me what my book would be about: A woman who was doing things, a woman who was dedicated, a woman who could do it all – and did!

It was clear that I was drawn to this project from experience, interest and background. Through more than four decades of professional work, I have met the finest people who gave their time, energies and money to help others. But one woman stands out: Annette Shapiro.

Annette and I met many years ago when I was the professional fundraising director of the Woman's Division, the United Jewish Fund, San Fernando Valley and she was the volunteer leader. I had the privilege and joy of working with her on many projects; I had the pleasure of seeing her grow and reach out for more challenges and more service.

Through the years, we have been friends, and when it came time for me to write my book, the person who met all the qualifications was Annette.

Our relationship has been a joyous one. All doors were opened. Family and friends were eager to help; they were conscientious in providing the observations and experiences that brought additional insight into Annette's special personality and accomplishments. As I researched and interviewed and wrote, I soon learned that Annette herself was the real story – her enthusiasm and her excitement, her dedication to family, to life and to the community. *She* is this book's story. This is Annette!

Throughout my work on this venture, which deals with people and their needs, aspirations and goals, I have been supported by my husband and my partner for the last fifty years, Daniel Harris. He inspired me, cajoled me, and helped me with details large and small.

My son, Alan, and his wife, Rae Ann, and my grandchildren, Jacob and Deborah, were always there, following my progress and encouraging me along: "How's the book going, Mother?" "When is it going to be finished, Grandma?" Their words of encouragement and interest are what kept me going.

My dear friends Gerda and Kurt Klein were involved through every stage of the project, and I thank them sincerely for their confidence, interest and inspiration.

Dr. Jack Shechter, Dean of Continuing Education at the University of Judaism, was a facilitator and a friend to both Annette and me, as he counseled us on the needs and merits of "our book."

To the many other good friends and advisors: Thank you for your interest and confidence.

As someone once wrote, the different between writing a book and thinking about it are these two words: "Doing it!"

Goldye Harris

ONE

WHAT IS A PROFESSIONAL VOLUNTEER?

What is a professional volunteer? The person with the expertise to answer the question – and the person who best exemplifies the life and career of a "professional volunteer" – is Annette Familian Shapiro. Throughout the pages that follow, Annette will share her wisdom, experience and inspiration about volunteerism. But the first question that Annette answers is the most fundamental one: What does it mean to be a professional volunteer?

Volunteerism is an old and honored tradition in America, and nearly one hundred million Americans volunteer their time, effort, talent and money to various causes every year. For some, it's a matter of dropping off a bag of groceries at a food bank, or addressing envelopes, or chairing a meeting, or writing a check to a favorite charity, or dressing up for an evening at a gala benefit. But for others, volunteerism is their life's work – that's what I mean by a professional volunteer.

The professional volunteer, no less than a doctor or a lawyer or a teacher, is pursuing a career. Like someone preparing for one of the other professions, she/he must learn how a charitable organization really works, how the volunteers and professional staff interact with each other, how fundraising dollars are turned into programs and services. The professional volunteer holds a "doctorate" from the "school of volunteerism."

Professional volunteers, like other professionals, must "pay their dues" by accepting "entry-level" responsibilities in a charitable organization. As they grow and develop, the work becomes more challenging and more responsible.

A résumé is important to the professional volunteer even as it is to the upwardly mobile business executive – and she/he will make an effort to seek out a variety of projects and tasks so that his or her résumé will show breadth and depth of experience.

Doctors and lawyers put in long hours, and their private lives are often interrupted by the demands of their patients. The same is true of the professional volunteer, whose evenings and weekends may not be their own. She/he is truly "on call" at all times.

Volunteers, of course, are not paid for their services, at least not in money. But there are other measures of worth and other forms of compensation. Nowadays, we hear much about the need for "psychic income" in the workplace, the need to feel that one's job makes a difference in the real world. The professional volunteer is richly paid in this "psychic income," and understands that long hours and hard work make a difference. One can see what they accomplish in the faces of the men and women and children who benefit from the programs and services of the organization which one serves.

Why do women and men choose to dedicate themselves to service as volunteers? Because it is a career and way of life with its own rewards and satisfactions, and it's an honorable way to put one's talent and energy to work in the service to the community while, at the same time, meeting the many challenges of home and family.

Indeed, I believe that the professional volunteer is actually a better spouse, even though the family is often called upon to share with the community. Such a person is fully alive and energized by his or her work, and enjoys a sense of self-worth and fulfillment that shines through the stresses and burdens of everyday life, and is a wonderful role model for spouse and children, friends and relatives.

Above all, the professional volunteer is connected with the world in a dynamic and rewarding way: working with energetic and exciting people, solving problems and meeting challenges in a dozen different ways. And, every day, the professional volunteer makes an impression on the world – by helping others, by building and developing the resources of the community, and by showing the world what can be done.

If this sounds like a "true believer," it's because I have lived the life of the professional volunteer, and I know first hand what a beautiful and fulfilling life it can be. Whenever I am asked the inevitable question – "And what do you do?" – I proudly answer: "I am Annette Shapiro," and I hand them my personal calling card that reads:

A N N E T T E   S H A P I R O
PROFESSIONAL VOLUNTEER

TWO

THE FAMILY

Behold how good and how pleasant it is for brethern to dwell together in unity.

Annette Familian Shapiro was born in Los Angeles, California, on April 17, 1930, to George and Rosella Familian. Hers was a family of doers, a family devoted to creativity and philanthropy, and she grew up with her brother, Arnold, in a household where the troubles of the day did not dampen an optimistic spirit.

According to the Los Angeles Times (Circulation: 9,300), the day of her birth was balmy and smog-free. Headlines announced that the United States, Great Britain, and Japan had pledged to make cuts in the world's largest war fleets. The city's new airport, built at a stupendous cost of one million dollars, was hailed as the aviation center of America. By comparison, the budget for the newly-released "All Quiet on the Western Front" was two million dollars, and The Times proudly announced that every picture now being filmed in Hollywood was "talking."

Claudette Colbert had just arrived in town to make her first "talkie," and a new picture starring Al Jolson was in the works: "Mammy". The best seller list included "The Door" by Mary Roberts Rinehart, and "Judy" by Faith Baldwin. An ice cream shop that had sold its four millionth cone was in the news, and so was a small item predicting that baseball games would be seen and heard by means of something called "television" within the year.

A home on South Almont Drive in Beverly Hills – including two tiled baths and a picture window – was listed for $9,950, and a Chevy Sports Roadster was advertised at $550. At the Piggly Wiggly grocery chain, lamb roast was selling for 29 cents per pound, eggs for 27 cents a dozen, and asparagus at ten cents per pound. A round-trip tour of Canada, the Rockies and the national parks was advertised at $120.

Of course, the next two decades would include the darkest years of the Depression, World War II and the Holocaust. Every American family, every Jewish family, was confronted with terror and tragedy. But Annette and her family emerged into the brave new world of postwar America with high hopes and bright dreams. For Annette, the dream of putting herself to work in service to the community was destined to come true.

Heritage

David Familian, Annette's paternal grandfather, was born in Russia in the town of Skiva. In 1903, at the age of 21, he came to Philadelphia as an immigrant. There, he reunited with a Russian family by the name of Brilliant, which had arrived prior to his arrival. Celia Brilliant was his beau in Russia, and Celia and David married and had four children – Lillian, Al, Isadore and George. George Familian was born in Philadelphia. The family moved to Los Angeles in 1910 and settled in Boyle Heights.

The Familian family was among the pioneer philanthropists of the thriving metropolis, and it is their legacy that inspired Annette.

"Jewish immigrants like David Familian brought a tremendous drive," explained Rabbi Aaron Wise, of Adat Ari El in North Hollywood, California, at a memorial tribute to David Familian in the chapel that bears his name. "They possessed a basic elemental force, strength and a faith, a power of positive living that was truly remarkable. They were not 'fazed' by the New World. In business life, in the marketplace, in the union halls, they were imaginative and industrious, they were fighters, and they carved out for themselves and for us a place on the American scene. Their dynamism can be compared to the spirit which the Jews brought to the Land of Israel when they transformed it into the present state."

David Familian's sons, George and Isadore, followed in their father's footsteps, both as business entrepreneurs and as champions of every humanitarian and Jewish cause. Although neither of the brothers finished high school, each one made a mark in an industry that was crucial to the explosive growth and development of Southern California. George, Annette's father, worked tirelessly until his death in 1959 to build Familian Pipe and Supply into one of the largest plumbing wholesalers in Southern California.

George met his future wife – Annette's mother – when Rosella Moldovsky, the only child of Ida and Isaac Moldovsky, was only 14 years old. George and Rosella, a native-born Angeleno, were married in 1926, and they moved to the San Fernando Valley in 1938, where they were among the pioneers of the Jewish community. They joined the first congregation in the area, Valley Jewish Community Center, and devoted their energies to building the congregation into the synagogue that is now known as Adat Ari El.

"There were lots of meetings in our home as Annette was growing up," Rosella remembers, recalling Annette's childhood in the house that Rosella designed. "We believed that unless you do the things that need to be done, they just don't happen. So we guided our children in what we considered to be the 'right' way, and we made sure they had opportunities so they wouldn't come back and say we didn't give them a chance."

George and his brother Isadore were partners in Familian Pipe and Supply and Price Pfister Brass. All during their business careers, David Familian, the family patriarch, impressed upon his sons that the family should look to the future with a sense of responsibility and a generosity of spirit.

New Californians

Bertha and Fred Shapiro arrived in California on New Year's Day in 1928, and lived for a short time at 31st and Avalon in Los Angeles. Later, during the Depression of the 1930s, they settled in the community of Sierra Madre. Their first son, Leonard, was born in 1928, and Bernard came along two years later. The times were difficult, and so the boys helped out their father after school at the family jewelry store on Hill Street in downtown Los Angeles, and they learned basic lessons from their parents.

"I was raised with a *pushke*," Leonard says of the small metal box that is a fixture in many Jewish homes. "We always kept it in a prominent place in our house to collect money for charity. In fact, my father attached a *pushke* to the back seat of his car; he drove six people to work every day, and they were expected to put money in that *pushke*."

Bernie played a crucial role in Leonard's life when he uttered the familiar words: "Do I have a girl for you!"

Leonard was skeptical – but his younger brother was right. The girl was Annette Familian, and Leonard met her on a December night in 1946 when the Junior Sportsmen of the City of Hope held a singles dance at the Hollywood Athletic Club, a facility that would later become the campus of the University of Judaism. Two years later – on April 4, 1948, when Annette was a senior at Fairfax High School in Los Angeles – Leonard and Annette were married.

"Teenage brides were rare in those days," Leonard recalls.

"She was the only one in the school, and we had to get permission for her to remain after our marriage so she could graduate in June."

Not long after Leonard and Annette were married, Leonard joined Familian Pipe and Supply. About a year later, Bernie also came to work for the company. Some 12 years later in 1960, shortly after the death of George Familian, Leonard, Bernie and Annette's brother, Arnold, bought a part of the company from the family. By the end of their first year, the company had sales of $8,000,000. In 1965, Arnold sold his interest in the company in order to pursue other business activities.

By 1972, the company's sales had grown to $100,000,000 and the company was taken public as Familian Corp. With Leonard as Chairman of the Board and Bernie as President, the company continued to grow. In 1985, Leonard and Bernie purchased all the outstanding stock and took the company private.

By the time Familian Pipe and Supply was sold to an English company, Woolesly Ltd., its total sales exceeded $400,000,000.

Throughout Leonard's business career, he continued to be a community leader and a philanthropist in his own right.

"My boys have been in business together for more than 37 years and never had a falling out," Bertha Shapiro, of blessed memory, boasts. "Of course, I never would have allowed that!"

"Our family has always been close, and when my step-daughter Betty (the boy's half-sister) decided to move to Los Angeles, with her husband and daughter, the boys and their families prepared a real welcome. They rented and furnished an apartment for them, and gave them a new car."

A New Role

Leonard and his family played an important role in Annette's commitment to volunteer service. Bertha Shapiro recalls a meeting of Hadassah, the support organization for Hadassah Hospital in Israel, in the living room of Annette's home.

"They asked Annette to be president," Bertha recollects. "Annette wavered and said: 'I don't know.' "

"'Take the job!' " Bertha advised. "I explained that she would gain experience, and learn through doing. Most importantly, she had the time and the resources to devote herself to the work, and she knew other women in the same position who could help her." She accepted with Leonard's active blessing and Bertha's encouragement.

Both Leonard's and Annette's parents persistently encouraged the young couple in their early involvement with community service. The Familians and the Shapiros had been supporters of the City of Hope when it was still primarily a hospital for the treatment of tuberculosis. Annette's grandfather, David Familian, had been one of the Founders of the institution and Annette and Leonard followed their parents' example by becoming charter members of the Junior Sportsmen and the 500 Club, part of the fundraising organizations of the City of Hope.

Indeed, volunteer service has been an important theme in their family life. As Annette and Leonard grew up, married and raised a family of their own, they remained identified with City of Hope and the University of Judaism. In 1978, for example, Annette was honored by the Founders of the City of Hope at a testimonial dinner that raised more than $400,000 for the institution. In 1985, both Leonard and Annette were chosen as recipients of the Eternal Light Award of the University of Judaism, an honor presented by the Patrons in recognition of their long service to the University and its expanding programs and facilities. Leonard and Annette were Co-Chairpersons of the Council on Continuing Education, the lay leadership unit which guides the work of the University's renowned Department of Continuing Education (DCE). Dr. Jack Shechter, the Dean, was a great influence in getting Leonard and Annette involved with this educational work. Under the leadership of the Shapiros and Dr. Shechter, the DCE has emerged as the largest and most intensive Jewish Adult Education program in the country.

When the family was confronted by their son David's battle with diabetes, they were invited to join the Founders for Diabetic Research, a newly-formed support group for the diabetes program at the City of Hope. Annette and Leonard met with Dr. Rachmiel Levine, then the newly-appointed Medical Director of the City of Hope and a world-renowned expert in the field of diabetes.

"As time went on, we realized that we could not raise money for two separate groups for the City of Hope – the Junior Sportsmen and the Founders for Diabetic Research – without reducing our effectiveness at one or the other," Annette explains. "It was at that point that I associated myself with the American Diabetes Association."

Annette now emerged as a full fledged "professional volunteer"; this activity became an important part of her life, and she was supported in her work by Leonard. "I recognized early in our marriage that it was important for Annette to be doing something for others," says Leonard. "Annette's activities kept her life busy and interesting; she was learning a lot of new things, and she was never bored."

The Next Generation

Leonard and Annette have passed along their commitment to the next generation. David Shapiro, Joel Shapiro, and Ilyse (Lisi) Shapiro Teller were raised in a tradition of doing for others, a tradition that now includes four generations of Shapiros.

"People have said to me that our David, Joel and Lisi come by their feelings for charity naturally," says Annette. "My philosophy with our kids is: 'Do as I do – if you wish.' Each of them has brought his or her own personality to the family, and each one reacts according to his or her own interests. What they decided to do was their own decision, but each one felt a responsibility to get involved. This makes me very proud!"

The example set by their parents and grandparents was a strong influence on the children. "A family sets an example," Annette explains. "We sought to set ours; we are interested in community because Leonard and I believe that it is our responsibility to contribute to the community."

Annette imbibed as a youth the importance of setting an example – this one in connection with her Jewishness. She stayed out of school on Jewish Holidays and carried matzos in her lunch bag at Passover. She wanted to be counted, and felt it important to make a point that you, as a Jew, must respect who you are.

David, Joel and Lisi all share memories of a childhood filled with hard work and good times. "My attitude comes from what my parents did, not what they said – it just rubbed off on me," says David. "Our parents took us with them to help at events for City of Hope, Foundation for the Junior Blind, or whatever was happening. It was part of our growing up, and everyone seemed to benefit."

A surprise party for Annette on her 40th birthday had all the family involved; Leonard was chairman and committee members were David, Joel and Ilyse.

The announcement of the party was a beautifully scripted invitation which read in part:

World's greatest wife and mother
America's most fabulous friend
Los Angeles' most enthusiastic weight watcher
San Fernando Valley's "Sweet Charity Herself"

Since Leonard and Annette were both involved with the Jewish Federation Council of Greater Los Angeles and the United Jewish Welfare Fund, now called the United Jewish Fund, the party was held at "590 North Vermont," the former headquarters of the Jewish Federation Council.

Keeping the party a surprise was a major project. Leonard and committee devised a scenario which included a trip to

Las Vegas (which would also celebrate their anniversary) plus an emergency meeting at "590" the night of the party. It was a truly amazed Annette who walked into the entry rotunda and saw a crowd of family and friends shouting "Surprise! Surprise! Surprise!"

Two very useful and lasting gifts were presented. One was a solid gold whistle from her mother, which has become a trademark of Annette; the whistle has traveled all over the world with her. Its sound has alerted people to get on the bus in Israel, or that a meeting in Los Angeles is starting or dinner is served at her private parties. Or just (by now) the familiar sound that says Annette is here – let's make things happen.

The second gift was from Leonard. The meetings Annette attends usually include name tags. Leonard made it easy for her by his gift of a gold name tag which says "Hello, My Name Is Annette Shapiro."

Understanding

Joel and Lisi emphasize that Annette's commitments did not detract from the love and care that they enjoyed as children. "There were lots of meetings at our house when I was a kid," says Joel, "but I didn't realize how busy she was because she was always home when we got there." Lisi, too, feels that her parents' volunteer work only enriched her childhood: "I've never been resentful that my parents were involved in all their activities because I was brought up to understand the importance of helping others," she says. "I always got the attention I needed."

Above all, Annette and Leonard created a warm and nurturing environment in which their children enjoyed the attention of friends and family: "My mother is a very family sort of person," says David. "We had a huge circle of friends and family. A small party for Mom and Dad keeps growing, and one circle becomes many. She never wants to leave anyone out."

Annette and Leonard are proud of the commitment that their children have made to parenting, family and the community. David, as president of Familian Pipe and Supply, together with his wife, Lynn, have been involved in the American Diabetes Association, which supports research and programs for diabetes. Lisi, and her husband Steve, vice president of Shapco, Inc., are active in Concern II, a young adult organization that raises money for children with cancer. They were recently honored by this organization and received an outstanding leadership award. Both sets of parents are very active in their children's schooling and in the quality of their education. Joel, a physician, has been involved with Physicians for Social Responsibility and with issues of environmental concern. He is on the staff of an Urgent Care Center and volunteers his service at a local clinic. Joel also serves on the board of the Foundation for Transplant Research. In addition to his medical practice he has a great interest in acting and theatre.

"I see our family's involvement as bricks of commitment," explains David. "We start with one project – one brick – and as our activities grow, more bricks are added until we have a complete project. It's a good feeling putting those bricks of service in place, and seeing a project grow."

Opportunity From Adversity

No family is without its woes and worries, but Annette, Leonard and their children have learned from each problem that they have confronted. Leonard explains that it is important to have a healthy attitude toward making the best of life's opportunities, even in the face of adversity.

Leonard suffered a heart attack in 1972, and was hospitalized in Newport Beach for three weeks. "When I got out, Annette had rented a house in Newport Beach, and we stayed there while I recuperated," Leonard says. "It was a great three months – bicycling, exercising, walking every day – and we are still keeping that life style."

When the family returned to Los Angeles, Annette and Leonard moved into their new home in Beverly Hills.

"When we were trying to make a decision, a friend said: 'You've had a heart attack, and you might not be here next year – so you might as well buy it,' " Leonard remembers. "We've used that as a slogan ever since. We even named our boat "Might As Well."

When David was diagnosed as a diabetic at the age of 16, the family confronted yet another challenge. "We realized that nothing is permanent in our world," Leonard says, "You have to go along with the punches and overcome adversity and Annette and I learned this lesson and so did David. When I worked with David in our family business, I realized that our son himself developed the ability to deal with Diabetes while being a successful businessman."

David's physical condition – and his mother's example – also influenced his brother, Joel, who chose to practice medicine after his experiences in helping the family cope with David's health problems. "If every parent of a diabetic would work as hard for the cause of diabetes research as my mother," Joel observes, "God knows where we would be now." Joel has made the greatest commitment of all – he acted as an organ donor for his brother, who required a kidney transplant. Joel's kidney gave David a better quality of life for about six years.

Update: David and Ilyse

The family's strength, courage and love is tested again as David shows signs of rejection from the kidney transplant he received from Joel. Ilyse has responded to David's crisis with her decision to be the donor for her brother. She says: "I believe in the values my parents live by because they are right for me and my husband and children. David is my brother and I want to help him. My parents gave me the opportunity to be independent. Ours was a household of love, respect and caring. This is my way to show my feelings."

Annette continues: "Ilyse gave a kidney to David. Each time, waiting while my children were in surgery was hard beyond description. David, Joel and Ilyse set the example for me. Their courage showed me how we do what we must when faced with adversity.

I feel the pain that Lynn, David's wife, experiences each day with David's health problem. She truly is a wonderful wife and mother and sets an example for all of us. David has shown our family his strength in working through his health problems with dignity and hope. His brave and courageous manner in the way he lives his life gives me pride that never ends

The success of this transplant from Ilyse is providing David another opportunity for renewed health. Joel and Ilyse's decision to give a kidney to their brother, is uniquely their personal feeling of love for David. My thanks to Steve for understanding Ilyse's needs and to Lynn as she stands by David's side. As their mother, no words can express my feelings and my love."

Nurtured Relationships

Annette and Leonard regard their family as a source of pleasure and pride. They are attentive grandparents even with their busy schedules. Ilyse says: "My mom and dad enjoy being with their grandchildren, and continue to invest time and attention in their lives."

"Relationships with family members don't just happen," Annette reflects. "They have to be nurtured and cultivated-with a mutual sharing and caring. It is very important to always be there for each other in difficult times as well as good times. Above all, family is first priority."

When the pace of work is too intense, Annette and Leonard find ways to relax and renew their own relationship. Boating, biking and tennis are some of the sports that they share. And they find a special refuge in Palm Springs, where they enjoy a game of tennis, a bike ride, and casual get-togethers with their friends. We enjoy our life," Leonard says. "We like the formula we've worked out, and we have the freedom to live our slogan: "Might As Well."

THREE

VOLUNTEERISM:
THE BASIC ELEMENTS

B*eing a volunteer," says Annette Shapiro, "is an American privilege."*

Annette and I had been talking for about an hour, and she had already taken time to answer her tenth telephone call. The telephone conversations had ranged from social calls to intense discussions of an upcoming event, all part of Annette's "quiet" day at home.

There is an excitement about Annette's life because there is always something happening. Each time we sat down to talk, she was forced to borrow time from her duties and commitments to spend some time in reflective conversation about her work as a "professional volunteer."

My conversations with Annette amount to a graduate course in volunteerism, and I am pleased to share her words of wisdom here on some of the basic elements of that enterprise.

Why Is It Important to Volunteer?

Volunteering is a right that our society offers us, and it puts into focus the need to give time, service and money for social action and welfare services, health, education, the arts and other cultural activities. These would not exist to the degree

Leonard and Annette Shapiro

From left: Steve and Ilyse Teller, Joel Shapiro, Annette and Leonard, Lynn and David Shapiro

Bertha Shapiro

Fred Shapiro

George Familian

Rosella (Familian) Barbas

David and Lynn Shapiro

Joel Shapiro

Steven and Ilyse Teller

Natalie, William and Stephen Shapiro

Jordan and Courtney Teller

Erin and Ben Shapiro

they do now without the "free" time, effort and money provided by the public through the interest of volunteers.

I see American volunteers as a great gathering of people brought together in the spirit of caring, a group of men and women who want and need to be a part of something that is greater than the individual.

The rewards of volunteering are virtually unlimited. You are in a wonderful place – you are the one to call the shots, who works the hours that you want to work, who selects the organization to which you want to give your time.

It's also an excellent opportunity for you, your spouse and your children to be a part of the community. You can't isolate yourself or close your doors to the needs of society because the needs are your needs, too.

And the rewards can be very personal. Volunteering builds character, understanding and tolerance.

Does Volunteering Interfere With Work or Business?

Volunteerism can and very often is a boon to business and professional advancement. This kind of activity gives you an opportunity to connect with and expand your presence in the community. So while increasing your knowledge of social and personal problems and needs and honing your altruistic spirit, your network of associates in the community can lead to significant personal and professional growth.

An excellent example of skilled volunteers from the business and professional community is the "Loaned Executive Program", which has been a part of the volunteer scene for more than thirty years. The program includes men and women from finance, insurance, government, retail business, education, communications, industry and the arts, all of whom are "loaned" by their companies to serve on a once-a-year fundraising project.

The individual continues to earn a salary from the company while working for the designated organization. The volunteers apply their training and experience to the organization for periods ranging from three weeks to three months, and then they return to their regular job responsibilities.

The special skills and experience of the loaned executive are invaluable. Assignments may include organizing and conducting training sessions, person-to-person fundraising, chairing meetings, developing special communication materials; whatever the program needs, the loaned executive provides the talent and the time to move the project forward.

The executives, the professional staff, and the other volunteers often bond with each other in special ways. The executives develop a special identification with the organization. Staff and other volunteers develop a special working relationship with the loaned executive. More importantly, the community benefits because of the skills, talent and experience that are brought to bear on building a successful program.

Should the Family Be Involved in the Decision to Volunteer?

Of course, the decision to commit time and effort to volunteering involves your family. I'm fortunate in that my family is very supportive and interested in what I do. But I understand the situation of a friend of mine who was asked to take on an important chairmanship – and he turned the decision over to the whole family.

The vote was 4-to-1 to accept. The youngest son wasn't sure he wanted his daddy to be so involved because it might interfere with helping out the Little League team; after more family discussion, however, the vote was unanimous.

How Does an Organization Find – and Keep – Its Volunteers?

I have my own system for finding volunteers, keeping them interested and active, and matching them with the right activity for their skills and interests.

First, I like people. I'm really interested in them; they are important to me, and I'm willing to understand and respond to their needs.

How do I do this? I listen and observe until I feel I know the person well enough to find her or him a place in an organization that will meet his/her needs.

It's really a delicate process, and I work it very carefully. When I meet someone – or someone is referred to me – I discuss various tasks that may be projected for community organizations: fundraising, programming, education, and so on. If there is interest, I know that I've pushed the right button. I have been listening.

Then I activate my three-point program. I may make an appointment to talk more over lunch, or I'll send informational materials, or I'll schedule a tour of the agency in which they have shown an interest. This may be the beginning of a great experience – or it may also come to an abrupt end. Either way, I feel that I'm ahead and so is the person because they know more about the cause than they did before, and I still have the contact so if an event comes up that might interest them, I can send an invitation or make a personal call.

As a recruiter, I have an obligation to push, but a need to be sensitive when a person starts to pull back. I've learned the signs of rejection: telephone calls are not returned, mailed invitations are ignored, meetings are scheduled and then canceled – usually on an answering machine. A sensitive recruiter must recognize these signs, and move on to a new contact.

When all goes well, you have a new volunteer, and you know what you can reasonably expect from that person. But you still have to observe the strengths and weaknesses of the individual to find out where he or she will best fit in the available program. Remember, some people are really better and happier doing undemanding things while others wish to expand their activities and responsibilites. Accept their strengths, and don't push them into work which is inappropriate for them.

Remember, the needs of the community may be unlimited, but the volunteer work force is not. More demand and less people means that agencies and organizations are challenged to discover new and creative ways to find volunteers, including the use of direct mail, newspaper advertising, and even telephone campaigns. It is vital that agency professionals and professional volunteers realize that a volunteer these days is a rare and endangered species, and must be treated with tender loving care.

This means that volunteers should be happy and satisfied in their work. They should find it pleasant, rewarding and challenging within their needs and capabilities. If the experience of the volunteer isn't fulfilling, she/he will move on.

I have a theory that everyone cares – it's just that each person has a different way of showing it. For instance, I meet a family with a relative who is diabetic. I know they can identify with the American Diabetes Association on a personal basis, and so we have a common denominator to work with. It is then up to me to interpret and explain the best place for them to help. I can only do this if I have followed the most important rule of recruiting, and that is to listen.

Once a potential new volunteer has given me the answers, it's up to me to follow through on their interest. In most cases, people have been contacted many times before, but they have been turned off. I have the opportunity to renew the spark and start a fire in their imagination. So what I really am is a firestarter!

Satisfying Volunteers: Flexibility

Okay, so now you're a volunteer in an organization that has caught your interest. It even has an office near your home. You've attended an orientation session, and you've read their literature. You know the do's and don'ts. And, horrors, you find that you are not satisfied. What do you do now?

Speak up! Remember, volunteer work is negotiable and changeable. Find the area where you feel you'll be happy and effective. Jobs can be divided and partitioned in keeping with individual needs and interests. Don't forget that being a volunteer offers much flexibility. Find the right time and place for you. Don't be a martyr; if you're unhappy, don't grin and bear it.

Discuss your concerns with your chairman or the staff professional. Misunderstandings should be taken care of when they happen, before a project is too far along in its programming and scheduling. Be honest, and your volunteer activity will bring you all the fascinating and exciting goals that you envisioned. I know this from personal experience – it has and still is happening to me.

How Would You Summarize The Basics of Volunteering?

Four Phases of Volunteering:

1. **Knowledge** of what you are doing is a great asset in doing a better job and limiting your frustrations.
2. **Sensitivity** to the people around you and their needs will help you make the right decisions.
3. **Awareness** is knowing what is really happening around you in the organization.
4. **Listen** and **Transfer** what you hear to the right channels so that action can be taken and surprises kept to a minimum.

Remember that volunteerism is an important part of our country's unique heritage; it offers so many wonderful opportunities to everyone.

FOUR

WHAT IS A LEADER?

Annette's uncle, Isadore Familian, has described his niece's leadership qualities as a blend of heredity, the good example of her family, and her own unique gifts:

"Some of it is a spill-off from the family, but a lot of good things have occurred that are not a spill-off," says Isadore Familian. "Annette has felt the needs of the community; she knew she could be helpful; as time went on, she has motivated lots of other people, too. If you have the respect of your friends, you can be a leader. You are saying to the world: 'I believe in this.' When you say it strongly enough, your friends recognize the intensity of your involvement, and they become involved, too. That's what leadership is all about; leadership people are those who affect others."

Here is what Annette has to say about the challenges of leadership.

What Makes a Successful Leader?

A leader has many talents, but one of the most important is the ability to deal with people on a person-to-person basis and to understand their needs and goals. In fact, I believe that leaders usually evolve from what you might call "humble beginnings."

As an example, suppose you are asked to help on a committee. You are new to organization work, but you have a friend who is doing some work and said it might be fun if you helped. The project is a luncheon to raise money, and your job as reservations chairman seems easy enough and fits your time and interest.

You organize your time and get some pointers from an information manual that is given to you; everything goes very smoothly, and you enjoy your part of it, which includes making table assignments for each guest.

Of course, there are a few problems on the day of the luncheon when someone couldn't sit with one's best friend, but you managed to solve the problem by talking someone else into moving to a better seat so the two friends could sit together. In fact, you feel good about resolving the problem.

The group has an evaluation session after the luncheon, and you receive high praise for your poise and confidence. Your concern and friendliness, your caring and enthusiasm have been noted. You can hardly believe it, but you are asked to be the next chairman.

In Charge

You realize that leadership means that you will be in charge, and you will have responsibility for the whole committee. In this new capacity, you will work with the professional staff of the organization. You know that it would be helpful to have someone to go to directly with all your problems, someone who would be there to advise you.

But there are still other questions that you must consider and answer for yourself: What about the time involved? Can you pledge yourself to make enough time available to do the job?

Can you handle the possible responsibility of an increased financial pledge to the organization's fundraising efforts? It is the leaders who spark the commitments, including financial goals, for the groups that they lead. If there is a problem, it is important to discuss the issue with your spouse; you need support if you are taking on a major responsibility.

Other pertinent questions: Is this a comfortable place for me? Do I know enough people? Do I have enough influence? Can I get people to help me? Am I all that sure of myself?

The answers to these important questions will depend on many factors. But consider it to be a growing and maturing experience. There's an exhilirating thing about leadership: once you accept, you often find that you develop increasing confidence and you become aware that other people accept your leadership.

What Are the Most Difficult Challenges of Leadership?

It takes a certain amount of guts to be a leader, whether for six months, two years – or only one night. You have to be willing to put yourself on the line. But with good staff support, coordination, and the teamwork of a committee, it is all possible.

Especially important to the success of a leader is the help that you can expect from the professional staff. The staff is there to facilitate your efforts, to provide the continuity and experience that you need to fulfill your role as chairman. The role of the professional is extended and multiplied tenfold because of the volunteer leadership that stretches throughout the organization and the community. Learn to appreciate their role by keeping your "job" in perspective and making it work.

Believe me, the effective leader will attract volunteers. Leadership must be aware of the caliber of people in key positions. They are important links in the volunteer chain. If there is a breakdown, then it's up to the leader to mend them. And so a good leader is someone who puts one's personal ego needs on hold and is sensitive to the needs of others.

When you have a difficult volunteer – someone who causes discord, who doesn't follow through, perhaps even someone who is not fully truthful – it is still important to understand the individual's problems so he or she will not be disruptive of the group. And if someone repeatedly interferes with the goals of the group, then decisions must be made for the good of the majority.

Even when "enough is enough," however, it is very important to be a good sport. That's when I remind myself why I took the responsibilities of leadership in the first place. That clears it for me because I remember that the cause itself is what matters. That's why the frustrations in an organization take second place; I know the end result is so vital.

What Skills and Talents Are Necessary for Leadership?

As a leader, you must take the lead in setting the pace and goal for the workers.

Be organized. That means knowing the priorities of the project: scheduling, timing, recruiting, and goals. Charting can be an excellent way to see the total picture of volunteer involvement. (*See Pages 27*) And it is important to plan backwards: start with the date of the event, and move back in time from that date to determine when each task must be completed. (*See Page 28 & 29*)

Depending on the type of event – fundraising, educational or social – the chart is to be used for a timing schedule. Many groups begin the planning of next year's event the day after this year's program takes place.

Because of the intense competition for the time, attention and generosity of volunteers and donors, it's important to schedule an event so that it will not conflict with other fundraising programs. In many communities, there is a master calendar for social and fundraising affairs, and the event should always be placed on that calendar so that other organizations will know about it.

Keeping your own personal calendar current with your

organizational time schedule is essential, and a "tickler" file of important dates in chronological order is especially helpful. Suppose, for example, a volunteer requests that you call her after she returns from vacation; keep her name in the tickler file for the date when she is scheduled to return, and when the date comes up, you know that you must make the call. Of course, the effectiveness of the system depends on you; the file must be checked regularly and brought up to date when necessary.

The telephone is one of your best tools. It will be your direct line to your people, and you will know if a person is doing his or her job. There are some signals that help you to evaluate the volunteer: absenteeism at meetings, no telephone responses, excuses. As a leader, it is up to you to make changes before the problem becomes serious. Being a good sport or overlooking the danger signals is foolhardy; sometimes, you will end up being the one on the spot.

Be supportive and understanding, but read between the lines and cover your bases; there is more at stake than someone doing a bad job. Your organization's future can suffer. Be ready when weaknesses appear; take over, don't worry about hurt feelings at this time. Of course, you should do it in a way that spares the feelings of the person who is causing the problem; offer suggestions, not instructions. In most cases, however, the "problem" person will be relieved that you have come to the rescue.

How you handle problems reflects your expertise as a leader. Leadership is validating one's own response to the cause. Leadership puts a person in a position that makes a statement: "I'm ready. I want to succeed. Success is important to me."

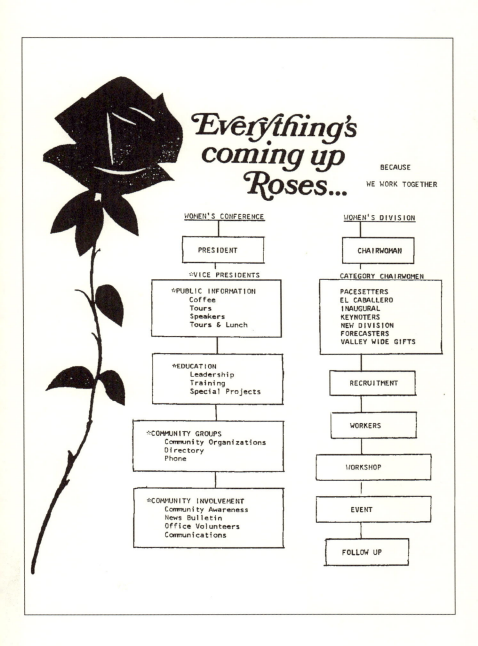

Everything's
coming up
Roses...

BECAUSE
WE WORK TOGETHER

WOMEN'S CONFERENCE

PRESIDENT

✫VICE PRESIDENTS

✫PUBLIC INFORMATION
Coffee
Tours
Speakers
Tours & Lunch

✫EDUCATION
Leadership
Training
Special Projects

✫COMMUNITY GROUPS
Community Organizations
Directory
Phone

✫COMMUNITY INVOLVEMENT
Community Awareness
News Bulletin
Office Volunteers
Communications

WOMEN'S DIVISION

CHAIRWOMAN

CATEGORY CHAIRWOMEN

PACESETTERS
EL CABALLERO
INAUGURAL
KEYNOTERS
NEW DIVISION
FORECASTERS
VALLEY WIDE GIFTS

RECRUITMENT

WORKERS

WORKSHOP

EVENT

FOLLOW UP

Your Future Looks Great!

CAMPAIGN TIME SCHEDULE

PLANNING	JOB	YOUR DATES
Aug., Sept. Oct. - Dec.	Organization Meetings	_____
	Committee Meetings	_____
	Letter to Workers	_____
	Upgrading & Assignment Selection	_____
	"Coffee & Conversation" (training - education)	_____
	Tours	_____
	Tours & Lunch	_____
	Assignments - Workshop	_____
	New Prospect - Researched	_____
	Recruitment	_____
3 Months Before Event	Review Pledge Cards: Upgrading-Rating	_____
	List of All Workers Names Turned In	_____

CAMPAIGN TIME SCHEDULE

CAMPAIGN BEGINS

PLANNING	JOB	YOUR DATES
6-8 Weeks Before Event	Division Meeting	_____
	Assign Special Cards	_____
	Cards Assigned to Typing Committee*	_____
8 Weeks Before Event	Invitation Copy for Luncheon	_____
	Publicity for Event	_____
	Instruction Sheet	_____
5-6 Weeks Before Event	Notices for Workshop	_____
	Prepare Kits for Workshop	_____
3-4 Weeks Before Event	(1) Workers' Meeting—Distribution of Kits	_____
	Set Dates for follow-up Phone Sessions	_____
	(2) Mail Invitation to Luncheon	_____
10 Days - 2 Weeks Before Event	Contact All Workers	_____
	Phone Session if Attendance Low	_____
	Plan Final Meeting for Luncheon	_____
DATE OF EVENT:	EVENT	_____
	Completed cards returned by Workers AND MONEY	_____
1 Week After Event	Report on Outstanding Cards – Start of Follow-up Phone Sessions	_____
2 Weeks After Event	Additional Follow-Up and Reports On Outstanding Cards	_____
4 Weeks After Event	ALL CARDS AND KITS SHOULD BE COMPLETED	_____

*If extra typists are needed, arrangements must be made four (4) weeks ahead by calling 786-4211 or 873-6811.

FIVE

WHAT IS A WINNER?

All kinds of pictures come into my head when I hear the word 'winner,'" says Annette. "It's like a kaleidoscope of bright people instead of bright colors, forming all kinds of patterns. And when all the bits and pieces blend together, it's a spectacular success."

Here's what Annette has to say about "winning" in the context of community service.

What Is a Winner?

A winner is creative, a self-starter, someone who can function alone, someone who has the excitement, enthusiasm and stamina to do his or her own thing.

A winner is an independent, a person who can almost single-handedly achieve the goals of a project. Winners are people with drive, people with commitment, people with goals, people who have strong ego needs and a sense of competition, people who want something so much or believe in something so ardently that they are willing to put their personal reputations on the line to make it happen.

A winner must also be a caring person, a person who believes in success and has the talents and skills to gain attention, a person who can motivate and challenge others as well as give his or her own unique touch to a project.

Many obvious winners come to mind in politics, arts, science and the sports world; that's because winners are competitive people who put their skill, training, determination and personality to work in order to meet the ultimate challenge.

Sometimes the ultimate challenge for a winner will be found in the realm of community service. It's a stratospheric place where the goals are high enough to present a challenge to even the most competitive person.

How Do You Spot a Winner?

The first time I meet someone, I judge him or her on appearance. I'd say much of the impression a person makes is a result of his or her appearance. Also, one's persona is reflected in facial expression: pleasant or harassed, calm or excited? These impressions make an impact on me; they say loud and clear: "I'm a neat, clean and pleasant person. I care about myself. I like myself; and so I'll care about the job I do."

For example, once I met a woman who made an immediate impression on me: "She's a winner!" I said to myself. So I made an appointment to have lunch with her, and her excitement, enthusiasm and interest confirmed my first impression. The next step was to bring up the project I had in mind, let her think about it, and then introduce her to our professional staff. The project was on its way.

Here are some additional guidelines for spotting a winner:
- A positive attitude (no matter what)
- The ability to work hard and consistently
- A good "salesperson"

Even a winner, of course, will have weaknesses as well as

strengths. Here are my observations on the characteristics, both positive and negative, that I find in a winner.

Strengths	Weaknesses
Wants to be in charge	Likes to do it "my way"
Strong point of view	Likes to work alone
Experience	Limited interest
Self-starter	Single-mindedness
Needs a challenge	

If the strengths are enough to counterbalance the weaknesses, then the signals are "Go!"

How Do You Work With a Winner?

Some winners find that working with others is drudgery because they have all the ideas and plans already outlined in their own minds. They tend to be very competitive; they have ego needs that makes it important for them to win. I have even heard such persons expressing frustration over working with others; it cuts down on getting the job done if they have to defer to other people.

So be it. What is really important is to understand how such persons work, and provide them with opportunities. This kind of winner will do best at a quick, limited project. The responsibilities for structure and continuity – recruitment, planning, and committee work, for example – should be given to others.

The person who is recruiting a winner should recognize the kind of framework in which such a person will be motivated to do his or her best. Usually, it's the "one-man job" that releases all his or her energy and focuses that person on the ultimate challenge. In a smaller project, the winner will most likely want to do all of the work, even the routine jobs such as phoning, mailings, making reservations, making seat assignments. That's how the winner maintains a sense of control.

Even when a winner prefers not to work with a group or a committee, the example of his or her hard work and success can serve as an example to others in the organization. The winner may have the social status or the name recognition that will be inspiring and motivating; the winner provides insight, experience, and a challenge to be more active, to be more committed, to be more generous.

Meeting a Winner

One never knows when that special person will come into your life. Leonard and I were invited to view the architecture of a home being remodeled. Upon meeting the owners, Dr. Patrick Soon-Shiong and his wife, Michelle, we found out that Dr. Soon-Shiong had been the first surgeon on the West Coast to perform three pancreas transplant surgeries (which cures diabetes).

We knew after several meetings that we had met a very special individual, a winner who is a gentle, dedicated, and caring researcher and doctor. Our impression of his potential for curing diabetes through encapsulated islet cell transplants was so exciting. As we built our relationship and understood what Patrick was doing in the field of diabetes research, we decided to take the lead and bring our family and friends together who were personally touched with diabetes. We were able to raise the money that gave Patrick the wherewithal to establish a laboratory with highly specialized equipment that would afford him the opportunity to move towards his goal of curing diabetes sooner.

The following invitation was the result of our efforts:

You Are Cordially Invited to the
Reception on June 8, 1988
Dedicating the Pancreas Transplant
Research Library
at the
Wadsworth Medical Center

Under the Direction
of
Dr. Patrick Soon-Shiong
Dedication by
Kenneth I. Shine, M.D.
Dean, UCLA School of Medicine
and
H. Earl Gordon, M.D.
Chief of Staff
Wadsworth Medical Center

Here are some of Dr. Soon-Shiong's comments about this venture interspersed with my reactions to his words, his deeds, his person.

Dr. Patrick Soon-Shiong: I really understood that the praise given at dedications is honestly earned, especially when describing the wonderful Shapiros. Those seemingly usual words – "great support" and "without your help" – took on new meaning for me when they were directed at Annette and Leonard.

The words became an important new truth for me because I really believe that without their help, great support and assistance, I would not have had the resources to build the Laboratory. They made the commitment to help, and now the Lab is completed.

I may not have given up without them, but I probably would not have had the time or the moral courage to go on with it because of all the stresses that are part of a fund-raising project. They understood my need to do something that I believe to be important. They have been wonderful, and I repeat that "without your help" I might not have gotten past all the frustrations. The Laboratory is my opportunity to work toward goals that are pure and beyond negative influences.

When I first met Annette and talked with her, it was like a dream come true. She was so enthusiastic and determined to help. It's hard for me to realize that in 1986, just a few years ago, the Islet program did not even exist, and the capsule technology didn't exist, but now it does. We have been in our Lab since March 1988; it is unbelievable what happened in such a short time.

Annette: In my many discussions with Patrick, I am impressed with his commitment to do something that is fulfilling to him as a surgeon, but also of great interest to him as a researcher. The problem we always face is the lack of money, and that is why we set up a non-profit and tax-exempt foundation to support this work.

Dr. Soon Shiong: The Shapiros have been so wonderful that I consider the Lab to be "The House That Annette and Leonard Built." A plaque with these meaningful words hangs on the wall of the Laboratory, which was dedicated on June 8, 1988:

> *In Appreciation of Annette and Leonard Shapiro, Whose Generosity and Support Were Invaluable in the Development of This Pancreas Transplant and Diabetes Research Laboratory. Their Commitment Is An Inspiration to Us All.*

Annette: Admiration is a two-way street, and it's really been a proud and special privilege for us to have been a part of this beginning with Patrick.

Dr. Soon Shiong: We have achieved major advances, bringing us closer to our goal of transplantation as a potential cure for diabetes. The continuing research brings us closer to the clinical trials where we hope to offer the first transplants to diabetic patients. I want this completed so I can do something for other diseases that need to be conquered.

Annette: Patrick shares the commitment to finding a cure for diabetes mellitus that brought us together in the first place. I realize that there is always work to be done because there are so many "firsts" in diabetes research that are yet to be achieved. We look forward to the first transplant before the year 2000.

I know Patrick is a winner. In my experiences with involved and dedicated people, I feel we all have a winner hidden somewhere in our beings. It just takes an intensity, a sense of purpose and an attainable goal to bring it out.

To quote Leonard: "Research is like a pyramid; it starts at the bottom with research from all over the world, each one contributing his or her knowledge and expertise. The answers begin to narrow as they approach the medical solution. It takes mutual understanding and great skill, and dedication, to get results. We feel that if there is a cure, Patrick got us onto the right track."

Update: May 6, 1993

The first human encapsulated islet cell transplant was performed by Dr. Patrick Soon-Shiong of the National Institute of Transplantation at St. Vincent Medical Center, Los Angeles, California.

The artificial pancreas was implanted in the abdomen of a 38 year old man who has been diabetic for more than 30 years.

"This is really exciting; we've been waiting for this for years." a spokesperson from the National Institute of Diabetes and Digestive Diseases said.

Annette: I sat in the lobby of St. Vincent's Medical Center waiting for Leonard and Joel. Together we met the first human that received the cell transplant, Steven Craig.

When Patrick introduced us to him we were warmed by his friendliness and appreciation. He explained that he had just had a meal without insulin and feels good. It was a proud moment for all of us, realizing that we were one step closer to a potential cure. We saw this as a door opening in the never ending battle against diabetes – one of the world's most heart-breaking and destructive diseases.

Update: January 24, 1994

Dr. Soon-Shiong performed his second islet cell transplant. The results of this transplant are very encouraging. Witnin five days Clarissa Hooper was totally off of insulin.

These are the first of 20 Federal Drug Administration approved implants being done for clinical trials.

We realize these two patients are clinical trials and our hope is that each of them will be off of insulin for a full lifetime, giving them a better quality of life.

SIX

GOOD JUDGEMENT

On a cloudy, dreary day in March, the fire burned briskly in the bedroom fireplace, casting a cheery glow on the chintz sofa cushions. Annette's sitting room/bedroom was a cozy place to chat as we sipped cups of steaming coffee, and tried to ignore the fresh pastries on the coffee table.

"Good judgement is really a fascinating subject," she remarks, "but I would define it as recognizing the truth when there seems to be more than one choice. It takes wisdom and understanding to come up with the best solution."

Here is how Annette has practiced good judgement in her own life.

An Example

The first and most memorable occasion when we were called upon to make a good judgement call happened many years ago when I was president of the Valley Guild for Children, an organization that raised money for the Foundation for the Junior Blind. It's strange, but I see it as if it were yesterday.

I called a meeting of our committee at my home in Encino, and we were all seated in the den. No one was smiling or chatting; we all felt down because we knew that we would have to make a decision that could affect the future of the Guild.

We were planning to hold our major fundraising event, a dinner dance with the theme of "La Bal Cirque," as an outdoor event at a private home. It was April, the ticket sales were slow, and the weather was very uncertain. Should we invest in a tent, and not worry about the weather, even though it would be a sizable expense and we might actually go into debt? Or should we cancel the event and try again later when the odds were in our favor?

We decided that taking the risk of renting a tent would be too expensive – and we could lose money on the event. So we canceled La Bal. It was a painful for all of us, but it was the right decision, because the Guild went on to do great things.

What made the difference was the ability to look at the situation honestly. People do not like to go to an event that is a dud. They like to think of themselves and their work as a success. So if an event or a program is going to be too destructive psychologically, and too costly financially, then it's okay to cancel and try again.

Good Intentions Are Not Enough

The best intentions of good-hearted but unknowledgeable people are not enough. I recently read about two leaders who wanted to help their hometown create a program for children. They proposed a fundraising concert. Everybody was in favor of the idea and said they would help, but when they were actually asked to do something, they weren't available. The City Council and the officials who approved the event didn't buy tickets. On the day of the concert, one of the performers took a look at the small crowd and canceled his act. To make it worse, the leaders were stuck with costs totaling more than $1500 while revenues were less than $500. It was a sad story – but it can happen when you keep thinking that everything will work out even though the facts are screaming at you that it can't.

The lessons are clear. Begin your recruitment when people are excited and you have face-to-face contact. Ask for a specific commitment – a general agreement or a vague approval is asking for trouble later on. And be alert for danger signs. When the members of the City Council did not bother to buy tickets, it was a definite sign of trouble ahead. If the leaders had recognized and heeded the danger signs, they should have canceled the event and tried again.

A failure of this kind has repercussions that go beyond the event itself. Volunteers are hard enough to find – and a negative experience will only drive the less committed ones away. However, even a negative situation can be turned into a positive learning experience if it is understood that it is sometimes necessary to reevaluate a project that has failed. Then everyone can move ahead to a more positive experience.

Turning Adversity to Constructive Channels

Sometimes even a heartbreaking experience can be an opportunity for growth. Since we first discovered that our son, David, had diabetes at the age of 16, the need to help find a cure for this terrible disease has changed our lives in many ways, and brought a new dimension of interest and awareness to our whole family. When I talk about what I'm doing in the area of diabetes research and treatment, it's amazing how many people want to get involved and need to get involved. Yes, the terrible difficulties and adversities can be turned into powerful motives for good and can bring others into the process of making life better.

Friendship

When you enter into a friendship with other persons, you are exposing yourself to their problems and concerns as well as sharing the good times. It is important to be aware of your friends' lifestyle and interests. When people do not give to a cause important to me, I realize that they may have their own causes and concerns. I do not want to lose friends because they do not respond to my personal request for contributions to the charities with which I have chosen to be involved.

The same thing is true when you encounter people as the leader of a volunteer organization. You must be alert to their problems and concerns, especially when a personal problem intrudes on one's responsibilities in a volunteer organization, and you must make room for the individual to make a commitment that is comfortable and appropriate in their present situation.

Just such a situation presented itself when one of the chairmen for a fundraising drive was having personal financial problems. He came to the leader of the group to discuss the best way to volunteer since he could no longer make a financial commitment. The leader was most insensitive, and told him that it was better for him to resign. The chairman, of course, was very unhappy because it was important for him to feel that his efforts were still needed.

That's when I got involved. Fortunately, the chairman came to me with his problem before he was totally lost to the organization, and I rescinded the earlier suggestion. That wasn't an easy thing to do, but the suggestion that the chairman resign showed a lack of sensitivity and insight. My suggestion gave the chairman a chance to serve a cause that was personally important to him – and it gave the organization a chance to show that we cared about people and their feelings, not just their money. As a result, we saved a volunteer worker, made a friend, and – only a few years later – we found ourselves with a top contributor!

Common Sense and Compassion

The emphasis should always be one of common sense and compassion. When dealing with volunteers, rules and regulations must be flexible.

For example, I encountered a woman with a diabetic

child. The association asked me to call her to offer information and assistance. Well, I made three telephone calls – and left my name on her answering machine each time – but got no response. Finally, I said to myself: "Annette, what are you doing? If this woman wants to call you, let her do it." So I called the person who had given me her name and said: "Look, she probably doesn't want my help, and pushing is an imposition, so that's all I can do right now."

About a week later, I finally got a call from the woman I'd been trying to reach. I found that she was really interested in the work of the association; she asked me a lot of questions, and we made an appointment to meet the next morning for coffee. Once I let her know that I was only a phone call away, I left it to her to take the initiative. When she finally decided to call me, it was her decision.

SEVEN

THE BOARD MEMBER

In art we have inherited a wealth of work
Which inspires and delights.
Theories and ideas continue to enhance
But the work is not completed on canvas –
It is completed in the mind of the viewer.
So, too, is a board member whose thought and
action direct activities to enlighten and serve.

"Being a board member is one of the highest priorities and privileges on my personal agenda," explained Annette, smiling at Leonard as he seconded her statement with a firm: "Yes!"

Then, in a thoughtful mood, Annette gestured toward the latest acquisition in their collection of modern sculpture. "I must tell you that our sculptures have given us some special feelings that bear on a discussion of our service on various boards."

Annette continued: "The sculptures offer different insights and emphasize different moods, depending on the viewer. That's why we're so excited about modern art; it can have a totally different meaning and feeling for each person, depending on a person's outlook or mood.

"The sculpture at the far end of the terrace outside our bedroom door is fun and whimsical and so vivid; it shows the fun side of life.

"Then the sculpture titled 'Reflected Attention' is so strong and large and colorful, with its bright red panel standing like a silent sentinel, that it gives off a feeling of power and authority.

"And then there's the sculpture called 'Durban'; I find it soothing and peaceful. It's so calm with its huge smooth rocks, and it describes the way I feel about Palm Springs: the desert is relaxing. A different world for me."

"Palm Springs is a different world for me, too," adds Leonard. "I remember my first trip there before we were married. Annette's folks invited me up for the weekend. My car was so old and beat – no way could we have driven there! So we took the train. The folks picked us up at the station. I wore my good double-breasted pinstripe suit. Everybody else was in white jackets and light pants. Everyone seemed so rich; it was a major cultural shock for me."

Leonard continued: "At the beginning, I had difficulty in dealing with it. That lifestyle seemed overwhelming for a twenty-year-old fellow from a conservative Jewish family in Sierra Madre. Then I reasoned that my in-laws also had come from humble beginnings, and they did not have trouble dealing with the good life. So I would learn how to handle it, too!"

"And you have," said Annette, laughingly.

"Our first introduction to art was also memorable," Leonard added. "We had just moved into our first home, which we bought with $6,000 borrowed from Annette's parents. We didn't know from art, and even if we had known something about art, we didn't have the money to buy it. However, a friend who was going through our new house was shocked that we didn't have any pictures, and he insisted that we borrow a picture from his collection. We did –

and we liked it so much that we wanted to buy it. When he said no, it wasn't for sale, that was the push we needed to begin our own art collection. We have discovered how much fun it is and what a great dimension of interest and adventure it has added to our lives."

"And now back to the subject," Annette interjected, "before I forget the point I want to make. Sometimes I see the people who become members of boards of directors – with their varied backgrounds and special expertise – as a group of artists bringing their best input to create an exciting structure for the expansion of the organization. I suppose that's why there are so many ways of recruiting board members; and the various approaches are as different and contradictory as wonderful works of art."

Peer Validation

I'll start with the most positive aspect of becoming a new board member. Suppose you are a volunteer for an organization; you give money, you participate in its projects and events. You have been active for many years; and now you are asked to serve on the board. To you, this is the ultimate validation. You are being asked to be where the action is, where decisions are made, and where the real guts of the work is decided.

Of course, not every new board member is a seasoned volunteer who comes to the job with a firsthand knowledge of the organization. Because of shortages in volunteers, some organizations may pick board members by "fishing" – throwing out the bait and hoping for a good catch. The candidates for board membership may be invited to join the board for a number of reasons:

- The person has not been involved in the organization, gives a minimal contribution, and shows only limited interest. Still, friends who serve on the board feel that the person has potential as an active volunteer, and so contact is made.

- The person is a large contributor, and the nominating committee feels that someone who gives so generously would be an asset to the organization.
- The person has been a leader in another group but has given to the organization. Leadership qualities are always in demand, and the nominating committee reasoned that the person might be ready to expand his or her interests to include the organization.
- In these times of mass communication, an advertisement in the newspaper giving a list of volunteer opportunities, including board membership, may attract the attention of a qualified candidate.

Now you know how you came to be considered for board membership. Here is how you may be approached:

- A letter requesting your participation on the board, and a return card for your response.
- A personal call from a board member with an invitation to meet for information and discussion about board membership.
- A telephone call with a promise to send a letter with more details.

Of all these approaches, the best is a personal call followed by a face-to-face meeting. You have now done your job. Now it is up to the candidate.

Asking the Right Questions

My advice to the perspective member is to consider the organization and the demands of board membership in regard to her or his own needs and interests. Keep in mind that board membership in an organization is a commitment to attend meetings, give money, and stay involved with the organization's programs and projects.

While board membership is certainly an honor, there are certain risks involved. You are vulnerable to criticism because you will be called upon to decide how to spend donated or public money. You are representing a group of people who need help. You are dealing with the lives of real people. And you work together with the professional staff.

As a board member, you are responsible for making informed and well-founded decisions about the funding and operations of the organization. So it is important to know the financial liability – if any – of unpaid directors of a non-profit organization. Although California law provides that a director who discharges his or her duties in good faith will not be liable for damages, many organizations also carry a liability insurance policy that protects directors.

A well-run organization or agency will have a plan to safe-guard employees, volunteers and clients, including maximum insurance coverage. The board of directors and its commit-tees will have competent professional advisors – attorneys, accountants, and other professionals – who will provide information and advice when called upon by the board.

A diligent board member will ask questions about all of these issues. Once your questions have been answered to your satisfaction, you will be in a position to fill the role of board member in a knowledgeable and effective manner. And I can promise you that board membership can be both an enlightening experience and a marvelous opportunity to serve the community.

The "Phantom" Board Member

Some organizations are content to have "phantom" board members who never attend a meeting. Personally, I do not feel that it is proper for an organization to just use my name on its letterhead if I don't know what they're all about. If stationery with my name goes out to people who know me, someone is likely to say: "Annette's on the board so it must be a reliable group." Your name on the stationery implies your approval of the organization, and so you must satisfy yourself that it is worthy of approval.

Then, too, the real value of volunteering is to make a

personal commitment. Being an active participant has put me in touch with outstanding professionals, and I have learned so much from them. Unless you are personally involved, you will learn nothing and you will not grow and develop as a leader. I really believe that I am able to present myself as a good leader because of what I learned by observing good professionals and lay leaders.

Of course, the same level of involvement may not be possible for everyone. But you must understand what is happening in the organization so you can ask the right questions. Such an effort is mandatory; if you can't find the time and energy to make that kind of commitment, you should think twice about accepting the responsibilities of a board membership.

Relationship to Staff

I have served on the boards of many different organizations for more than thirty years. I feel it is my responsibility to question how they handle their activities, who is directing their programs, what are the abilities of the executives and staff? And I'm not shy about speaking up if something disturbs me, or if I have an idea to share with the group. I may be wrong or I may have touched on something positive, and if the other members of the board agree, then it can be pursued and developed.

The role of the director includes setting the pace for growth and change within the organization. I've seen many changes in the staffing of agencies and organizations over the years, and I have come to realize how important it is for agencies to upgrade their staffs. This may increase the cost of operation, but it is vital if the agency is to meet the challenges of serving its clients.

I have a great respect for the professionals who work for educational, social, health and welfare agencies; they provide the continuity that is so important to the organization, both for its staff and its clients. A volunteer may be as active as he

Young Annette, 1940

Married, April 4, 1948

Young marrieds, early 1950's

Junior Matrons, Women's Division of The United Jewish Welfare Fund.
From left: Annette, Bebe Simon, Piper Laurie, Ruth Steele

Leadership, Women's Division of The United Jewish Welfare Fund. *From left:*
Annette, Betram Allenberg, Mrs. Freda Meltzer

The family at the dedication of the George Familian Research Building,
City of Hope

Leonard and Annette with Teddy Kolleck, Mayor of Jerusalem at United
Jewish Welfare Fund event

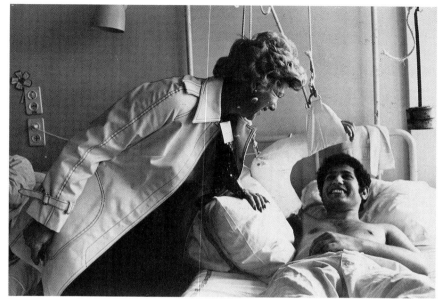

Annette carries encouragement from the Women's Division of the United Jewish Welfare Fund of Los Angeles to injured Israeli soldiers

Annette brings support to burn victim of Yom Kippur War

Annette and Goldye Harris are greeted by Col. Devora Tomer, Director of Women's Army Corp, Israeli Army

Annette as bus tour leader on trip through Israel

Annette at the Western Wall, Jerusalem

Sharing our visit in Israel with the elderly from different parts of the world

Annette with Bob Shriver, fund-raising for the McGovern campaign

Annette with Abba Eban, guest on behalf of the State of Israel

From left: Dr. Sherman Holvey, Annette, Gordon Stulberg and Dr. Paul Rudnick at an American Diabetes Association gathering in Annette's garden

Annette and Leonard receiving the Eternal Light Award from the University of Judaism. *From Left:* Dr. David Leiber, Annette, Leonard and Rabbi Aron Wise.

Annette receives the Most Outstanding Volunteer of the Year Award from the American Diabetes Association.

Annette presents a tribute to Ron Cey for his outstanding contribution to the American Diabetes Association as a Los Angeles Dodger.

Annette, Chairman of Community Dinner, United Jewish Fund, with Henry Kissinger and Sheri Lansing.

Yitzhak Rabin with Annette and Leonard at United Jewish Fund gathering.

or she pleases for a limited period of time, but the professional staff is there year-in, year-out to make the programs work even after any particular volunteer has moved on.

I believe that agency personnel should be paid fairly and in keeping with private industry. If this doesn't happen, good people will leave and programs will be hurt. Agencies are businesses, but they are businesses that give an opportunity for a better quality of life to the people whom they serve.

So when you serve as a board member, you must become a partner with the professional staff in the success of the organization. Speak up, be heard, show your concerns and interest! Do your homework. Use your contacts, knowledge and experience to extend the visibility and effectiveness of the organization. Take advantage of the marvelous opportunities for leadership and responsibility in this privileged position.

A Peak Personal Experience

My son David, because of his activities in the Amercan Diabetes Association, was asked to sit on the board of the Los Angeles chapter. In the reorganization of the California affiliates, the Los Angeles chapter of the American Diabetes Association was established. And, because of our involvement, we both served on the newly formed board of this chapter.

It was the first time we had ever served on a board together, and I was so proud of the way David handled himself at the first meeting. The next morning, I just felt compelled to write him expressing my personal pride.

I was proud, too, to see David put his talents to work at the board level. The board of directors of any organization is where the clout is, and where decisions are made that will affect the whole operation of the organization. It's the place that offers the greatest opportunities for service. It's hard work, of course, but it allows the volunteer to work on the inside of the organization. For me, it's an awesome feeling that I find exciting and exhilarating.

When you serve on the board of an organization, you're in the spotlight. You can't be overlooked. It provides an additional challenge because you know that your ideas will be heard by the "right" people. It's a good place to be if you have a project to promote. If you are serious about making changes in an organization, that's where you must be.

A board appointment is the peak experience of volunteer service, and it should be the volunteer's most rewarding achievement. The organization provides you with the tools: education, information, materials, training and meaningful jobs. But it's up to the individual volunteer to decide where you want to be and how far you want to go. Your acceptance of a seat on the board of directors is the start of a great adventure; make it work for you!

EIGHT

THE FINE ART OF NEGOTIATION

"*Negotiation is a way of clearing the air and clarifying the direction of a project," Annette observes. "Goals must be determined, and procedures must be outlined, whether it's a matter of raising money, promoting an event, training people, or initiating new programs. Simple? Easy? No – but those are the facts!" During one of our conversations, Annette shared her thoughts and experiences on the fine art of negotiation.*

"Now More Than Ever"

My philosophy is to create a better understanding among the volunteers and professionals who work together on a project. I always want to make everything "nice." I want everybody to like each other, and reach an agreement on what needs to be done. Obviously, it cannot always be achieved, especially in a group whose members have ideas of their own. But it's important to engage in open discussion about the pros and cons of a project before any plans are written in stone. That will enable the leader of an organization to work together and to meet even the most difficult challenges.

A friend recalls Annette's involvement in a major fund raiser for American Diabetes Association Diabetes research: "It was a small group of about eight people that Annette joined to plan the first premiere movie presentation in 1974. The film was "Towering Inferno.""

Her friend commented: "Annette is a key person. She is very sensitive and knows when to let leadership develop. A master fund raiser with a marvelous way of asking for money – aggressive but not offensive, she is respectful of people, and respects their time as well as her own. Through her dedication, committment and contacts her presence on the committee was responsible for raising hundred's of thousands of dollars."

Annette comments on this premiere venture: The premiere has always been successful, and the volunteers and committee membership looked forward to working on the event each year. Over the years, we have premiered such outstanding motion pictures as Towering Inferno – our first premiere – Barry Linden, Superman, City Heat, Hoosiers, Steel Magnolias, Beaches and many more.

However, the movie that we were supposed to premiere in 1985 was recalled by the studio for re-editing a few months before the event, and we were left without a movie to show! Our biggest fundraising project of the year – including the screening, an ad book, and a dinner – was suddenly in danger.

We met and discussed our options. Many different points of view were expressed, but we finally reached an agreement on how to proceed. We decided to send out an invitation to our customary guest list for the premiere, and invite them to support the organization even without a screening. Our theme was: "This Year We Need Your Help More Than Ever." And we succeeded in raising approximately $250,000 even without an event and no movie. Then we regrouped, we worked very hard, and the next year's premiere of Hoosiers raised more than $440,000, including $98,000 for the ad book.

Keep Cool and Stay Flexible

I urge people who serve on boards and committees to take the trouble to know the facts – pro and con – before attempting to conduct a difficult negotiation. They must also be sufficiently concerned to know and understand what the controversy may mean for the agency and its clients in terms of financial obligations and future commitments. In other words, be prepared, be motivated, and be persistent when you are called upon to negotiate.

Never forget that you may be facing rejection, and don't take the prospect too seriously. Keep cool, stay flexible, and "live to fight another day." Never, never put yourself in an all-or-nothing situation; if the negotiation doesn't produce the result that you believe is right, then maybe it's time to pull back and reevaluate the situation.

However, sometimes you find yourself dealing with a closed mind – someone who ignores the discussion of facts, shows no interest in change, and insists on a single perspective. In that case, there is a dilemma, and there may be no way you can reach the individual and change his or her mind. At that point, it is up to you to determine if your efforts will be more productive and more satisfying elsewhere.

A Most Unusual Man

I am reminded of a wonderful story about my grandfather, David Familian – a story that illustrates the limits of negotiation. He was a most unusual man, a philanthropist at a time when there were few people in the Los Angeles community who were equal to him in generosity and commitment. He really hated injustice, and he was concerned with the sick, the needy, the homeless, the aged, the oppressed, the refugees, and the pioneers in Israel.

During the Depression years in Los Angeles, the kosher butchers in the Jewish section of Boyle Heights raised their prices. Grandfather felt that this was wrong, but he could not get them to change their tactics even after many meetings and efforts at negotiation. So, as President of the Kashrut Board that monitored the dietary laws for the Orthodox community, he opened up a butcher shop and sent sound-trucks throughout the Jewish neighborhoods announcing lower prices for kosher meat!

Eventually, the pressure that he brought to bear on the kosher butchers prompted them to lower their prices, and business as usual was restored. Thanks to his efforts, he made it possible for many poor families to have the kosher meat that they could not otherwise afford.

Negotiations With Oneself

Of course, negotiations are a part of family life. I recall an incident when we were still kids at home; my brother Arnold, whom I adore, was upset with me because he said that I took over the bathroom. His form of negotiation was most effective; he made a point of getting there before me!

Then, too, we are always called upon to negotiate with ourselves over people, relationships, events, calendars, and commitments. I've said many times: "Annette, you can't do any more, you're already committed to a thousand things!"

But then another part of me will find a new concept or a new project so interesting that I cannot say no. I tell myself that it's a way to learn more, to meet different people. I like being friendly, I like to ask questions, I like talking, and I love the prospect of reaching out for new experiences. I never know where a new position or activity is going to lead me. It's like the beginning of a fascinating journey with a glorious treasure chest of experiences just ahead.

I suppose I take after my grandfather in my inability to say no. In 1942, the entire Jewish community in Los Angeles celebrated his 60th birthday, and there were sixty sponsors representing every part of Jewish life serving on the birthday committee. At the celebration, he shared his philosophy of life – and it describes my goal in life, too:

"Doing and giving and catching your breath," he said, "and giving and doing some more."

NINE

CONNECTIONS

The human race would perish from the earth if people ceased to bond to each other.

"Connecting people to each other or to projects or jobs is the greatest fun," comments Annette as she hangs up the telephone after another spirited conversation. "And the telephone is easily the best tool to 'reach out and touch someone' immediately. I enjoy connecting myself with somebody. And so my advice is: don't put off making a connection. It might change your life, or it might open some new avenue of interest; it's a continuing mystery and excitement to me."

Connecting with other people in a positive way is what the life of a professional volunteer is really all about. It's been said that it isn't what you know but who you know that counts, and there is certainly a grain of truth in that statement," Annette explains. "Connecting a person to a job, a project, or an organization is a link in a chain of relationships that may pay off in surprising and gratifying ways."

For example, Annette recalls talking to a friend who

needed a job. "I became the go-between – another link in the chain of relationships," says Annette. "I helped by putting her in touch with someone who could help her find a position. It didn't take anything from me except a telephone call and an idea about a potential employer who had a job opening for someone with her experience. But it resulted in a closer relationship, a sharing of resources, and a wonderful opportunity to help a friend."

Annette concludes: "Connecting is the key to the process of forging valuable relationships. And its the essential skill of a successful communicator. Keeping in touch with friends and acquaintances helps us create a network of people to call on for help with special tasks and projects."

Remembering

The connections that shaped Annette's leadership role began early. Rosella Barbas, Annette's mother, was active in a variety of organizations – City of Hope, Hadassah, Torah Fund, and Temple Adat Ari El – and served as chairman of many projects and events, but she never chose to take the presidency of an organization.

"I was too sensitive, too intense," Rosella explains. "Things worried me too much, and so if something wasn't being done, I would do it all rather than take a chance it might not be done right. Annette, on the other hand, could be president of three things at a time."

Indeed, one of the earliest newspaper photographs of Annette shows her as a seven-year-old volunteer filling holiday stockings given to needy children by the International Woman's Club. It was a foreshadowing of how Annette would connect to the community in dozens of ways through many different organizations.

"It's unbelievable," says Rosella. "I'm not known as 'Rosella.' I'm known as 'Annette's mother' – and I'm proud of it!"

Rosella recalls a memorable encounter between Annette and a woman whose daughter had been diagnosed as a diabetic. The woman called Rosella to ask for a referral to a doctor specializing in diabetes – and Rosella called Annette. "Of course, it was an emergency," Rosella says. "The family was in shock. Annette was on her way to a meeting with Leonard, but she responded immediately by meeting the family at the hospital. She was able to give them the name of a diabetic specialist, and she promised to return with more information about diabetes research, programs and activities in Los Angeles. The family was reassured, and Annette even made it to her meeting."

Annette emphasizes that diabetes comes first among her many commitments. "Diabetes is my first priority," she says, "and when I hear of someone who needs help, I make myself available to relieve some of their anxieties."

National Board

An exciting challenge presented itself to Annette when she was nominated to serve as a member of the National Diabetes Advisory Board of the National Institute of Health. She had prepared this personal statement in her application:

> My involvement with organizations concerned with diabetes began when my older son became a diabetic in 1967 at the age of 16. As a "Professional Volunteer" and a mother of a diabetic, I feel it is of utmost importance personally to support and have direct involvement with those organizations that provide research, education programs and treatment for those affected with this devastating disease.

There was no initial response. One of the most definite personality traits in this special lady is her persistence. This was out of her control and it represented unfinished business. A real no-no for this practical professional volunteer with a full calendar of projects. So this was put aside for more than a year – but not forgotten.

Annette met Henry Kissinger in April of 1985 and, as she explains, "He was so nice I decided to write him a note."

(*See Page 63*) "I won't say for certain that this had anything to do with my appointment; but what I want to bring out is that when you want to connect to something important to you, pursue it. Go for it. Someone will react."

In December she received the official notification from the Secretary of Health and Human Services inviting her to serve on the advisory board. (*See Page 64*)

"This appointment meant a great deal to me because I would be working on behalf of the research that was so important and could be the difference between life and death" Annette recalls: "I was very proud, too, because of the six members appointed from the general public in the country, I was one of the members who was a parent of a person who suffered from the disease."

The first meeting in January 1986.

"I arrived in Washington the night before the meeting and during the cab ride to the hotel we passed the National Institute of Health. Seeing that building gave me an overwhelming feeling of pride and awe because it was so wonderful to be part of a government that realizes the importance of volunteers and their ability to contribute something to alleviate a disease that affects so many people like my son David."

A few weeks later, a small group of family and friends got together for lunch to offer congratulations to Annette on her appointment to the National Diabetes Advisory Board. The group that gathered in the beautiful high-rise, glass-walled apartment viewed misty buildings and grey skies, a vivid contrast to the warmth and friendship that vibrated inside where spring flowers on pink and lilac cloths glittered with crystal, sterling and fine china. It was an Annette party, simple, light, friendly, a get-together of friends and family to talk with, listen to and enjoy. It was a beautiful picture of people together sharing their joy in honoring a very special lady.

When the goodbyes were given, a friend remarked:

"This has been such a good day for remembering that we were the people who through the years have been privileged to experience Annette's friendship and love."

Space in Our Togetherness

Arnold Familian, Annette's brother, explains that the connections within the family are important, too. "Our family connections are very close," he says. "Leonard and Annette, and my wife, Edith, and I make sure that our relationship keeps on growing. We recognize that life is not perfect – we've had our ups and downs and family traumas – but regardless of anything that took place, it never affected us. We would never allow it! Edith and Annette are like sisters, and Leonard and I are like brothers."

Arnold and Annette are still friendly with people that they first met at the original Junior Sportsmen's Group of the City of Hope that Annette joined as a charter member when she was fifteen years old, and when the Shapiros and the Familians attend fundraising events nowadays, Annette and Arnold are frequently the only "brother and sister team" in the room.

"Why?" Arnold asks. "The four of us work at making sure that the connections and the communication among us are open. We may not see each other every day, or even every month, but we talk on a regular basis. And if anything comes up that's a problem, we get it out and talk about it before it can becomes a serious issue."

Arnold, a calm, softspoken, agreeable man, reminisces about their father, George Familian. "He was a very sweet man," Arnold remembers. "He never yelled, never raised his voice. He was quiet and loving and would do anything for me, for Annette, for the family. I was in business with him for a number of years, and I think my personality as an adult is an extension of the way he was."

George Familian set a strong and enduring example for his family. "He was a good man – a lover, not a fighter – and that's the way he raised us kids," Arnold says. "He was also a great fundraiser, and stayed with the job until he got a check or a pledge. He worked as hard at charity events as he did at home and in his business. He never said 'no' to any good cause, and he was successful in business in spite of it. I remember his first heart attack – he was angry because it slowed him down!"

Isadore Familian, George's younger brother, also recalls George as a happy-go-lucky guy who had fun with his life. "We were in business together, we lived next door to each other, we were very close," Isadore says. "He had a feeling about life, and he had a lot to do with whatever I may be."

Annette's gift for making connections may be an inheritance from her beloved father. "Annette has the same involvement in charitable causes that our father did," Arnold explains. "I consider her as our family representative to the community. She is the most outspoken of anyone in our family. She has the capability and the need to serve the community, and thank God she is that kind of person."

Arnold proclaims himself to be proud of his sister's work as a professional volunteer. "It was great to see Annette in the middle of such big events as the Kissinger dinner. I was very impressed. Everything seemed easy for her. She knew all the right phone calls to make to the right people. There is no place or person Annette can't reach if she wants to."

Edith Familian, Arnold's wife, agrees with her husband's impression of Annette. "I have watched Annette's growth since she was 22 years old," Edith says. "Even then she was a magnet that drew people to her. She was a doer. Whatever she had to say, people listened."

Edith recalls how Annette set the pace for her own volunteer commitments. "Since I could not keep up with Annette in those early days, I always felt self-conscious around her," Edith explains. "I couldn't compete and I didn't want to – it isn't my style. However, Arnold and I have been involved in many great projects on our level. We are proud of her because we know that her enviable position is one she earned."

Annette's connections reach beyond her family, and extend into organizations throughout the community. "Annette's the kind of person who makes connections happen by talking first," explains one agency professional who knows her well. "She believes you can't know what people are concerned with until you talk to them. Annette is very straightforward and honest about describing her interests and involvement in diabetes. That kind of honesty can get other people to talk who otherwise would not acknowledge their problem. She has opened doors and allowed these people to connect with a group that can help psychologically. People learn that things are not so bad when they are talking with an interested and caring person like Annette – a person who has had similar experiences of her own."

Strangely enough, even Annette's commitment to dieting contributes to her effectiveness. "Dieting is a way of life for me," she explains, "and it organizes me in more ways than just eating less. It gives me renewed confidence, more self-assurance, and a real sense of being on track when I reach my weight-loss goal."

First Connection

On a typically busy day, Annette is going through the mail at her desk in a room that serves as office, file room and general workroom. That's where the connections are negotiated.

"I must get one thousand invitations a year," Annette says, displaying a handful of brightly-colored, attractive cards. "Of course, I can't go to most of these affairs, but I consider invitations as a method for an organization to establish a connection."

Annette holds up one of the invitations. "Look at this one," she says. "Someone has taken the trouble to write a personal note. That is so important, especially if the organization is new or the person receiving the invitation has been out of touch with the group for some time. A personal note from someone they know can make the difference about whether that person attends the affair, or the kind of contribution they will eventually make. Even if it isn't possible to add a personal note to each invitation – especially when hundreds may be going out – it's still a good idea to have a handwritten note photocopied and inserted into each invitation. You could send out a personal postcard a week after the invitation is received reminding them about your invitation and hoping they can participate."

The telephone, too, is an obvious means of connection. "In many groups I work with, each volunteer has a list of ten to twenty names of people who will receive invitations to an event," Annette continues. "They are asked to call those people who have not already responded by a certain date. This personal phone call can make a mildly interested person respond with a yes."

Connections have allowed Annette to grow and fulfill herself. "Since I am so concerned with diabetes and other organizations, it has given me many opportunities to grow beyond myself. I have connections within my own community, throughout the state and across the country, and as far away as Israel and the Continent. I understand myself better, and I have met wonderful, caring people. These people – whatever their background or age – share my concern for making our world a better, healthier place in which to live. I feel that the connections are just a beginning. The opportunities to enrich our lives are endless."

Annette Shapiro

April 29, 1985

Dr. Henry A. Kissinger
1800 K Street N.W., Suite 1021
Washington, D.C. 20006

Dear Dr. Kissinger:

Now I join the rest of the world in knowing how
great you are! What a privilege it was for me as chair of
the Los Angeles Community Dinner on April 16th for the
United Jewish Fund to share the podium with you. There is
not a day that goes by since that memorable evening that
I don't hear enthusiastic compliments. Your presentation
of the current world situation and your warmth and sincerity contributed so much to the social and financial
success of the evening. When you come back to our community
again to speak, I will make sure that it will be an event
as well organized as the one we just shared. (I look forward to that time.)

Your knowledge of diabetes research and your interest
in furthering this cause is so much appreciated. For this
reason I feel comfortable in asking for your help in Washington. Enclosed you will find correspondence that I have had
with the National Diabetes Advisory Board and my Resumé.
This is in response to my nomination from the American Diabetes
Association to this committee, which is part of the National
Institute of Health. The members of this committee will be
selected by Secretary Margaret Heckler some time in the middle
of May.

If it is possible for you to send a letter of recommen-
dation to Secretary Heckler I would be most grateful for
your assistance in this matter that is so important to me.

Warmest regards,

Secretary Margaret M. Heckler
Secretary of Health and Human Services
Room 615 F Hubert H. Humphrey Bldg.,
200 Independence Avenue S.W.
Washington, D. C. 20201

THE SECRETARY OF HEALTH AND HUMAN SERVICES
WASHINGTON, D.C. 20201

DEC 13 1985

OFFICIAL

Ms. Annette Shapiro
717 North Beverly Drive
Beverly Hills, California 90210

Dear Ms. Shapiro:

I am delighted to invite you to serve on the National Diabetes Advisory
Board of the National Institutes of Health, for a term beginning
immediately and ending September 30, 1987, subject to prescribed
appointment procedures and to periodic review of the Board's functions.

I hope you will find it possible to accept this invitation and give us
the benefit of your valued counsel. You may indicate your acceptance or
declination by signing and returning the enclosed Acknowledgment of
Invitation.

Upon learning of your acceptance, I shall ask the Director of the
National Institutes of Health to supply you with further information
relating to your appointment.

Sincerely,

Margaret M. Heckler
Secretary

Enclosures

TEN

GETTING IT ALL TOGETHER

Success is a science.
If you create the right conditions
You get the results.

Listen to what Annette has to say about this facet
of the professional volunteer's work.

In order to develop a project that is right for your organization, follow these important steps:

- Listen to what's happening in other areas about successful programs, activities, fundraisers.
- Determine if it is possible to recruit and build a volunteer committee.
- Contact a source which can sponsor an event.

We heard about a fabulous event that Neiman-Marcus had sponsored for one of the major health agencies.

The first contact was to set up an appointment with Neiman-Marcus. I was selected because of my successful involvement with the Premiere Committee. A meeting was arranged.

The N-M staff had questions of their own for me. Who

were we? What were our fundraising capabilities? I explained that our group raises urgently needed money for diabetes research programs and it has a record of successful fund raising events throughout the years. Neiman-Marcus was satisfied and our plans moved forward.

The event was called the "Great Catalogue Caper" because the fund raiser coincided with the kickoff of the world renowned Neiman-Marcus Christmas Catalogue, which is something of an event itself.

I felt confident that we could handle the project. In fact, I regarded the event as so important for us that I really put my credibility on the line. It was a wonderful opportunity, but it meant setting up an entirely new committee, recruiting new leadership, and – for me – it meant stepping aside and letting the committee "run with the ball."

One of the women recommended for the new committee had been very active in a number of other organizations. I telephoned her, and set up a luncheon appointment. I was very impressed with her personality, contacts and experience; I liked her and I thought she would be a perfect chair. She exuded a healthy self-confidence that would influence the other women in the group. The good feeling followed through to another meeting that I had set up with the executive director. It was a very "plus" meeting, and I was delighted when she accepted the task.

It may seem like a lot of work for a volunteer job, but our goal was to raise thousands of dollars in one evening. The success of the event would set the standard for other fundraising programs in the future. Most importantly, of course, the immediate goal was to raise money for furthering the diabetes research and programs.

The Neiman-Marcus project: The pieces come together

The very idea of the Great Catalogue Caper was something new for us. The evening promised to bring originality, prestige and a special visibility to our organization. We were at the crucial stage where we needed to grow and reach out. It would be our statement to the community that we were developing a different dimension and reaching out to a different audience. The Caper was the perfect answer.

The first meeting of the new committee was held in the Neiman-Marcus Tea Room. Everyone seemed to be delighted at just being there, and it was a wonderful feeling for me. People who might never become acquainted in any other way were now meeting each other and expanding their relationships. It was truly exciting for me to be a part of the scene, and I felt that we were really getting it all together – and getting off to a great start.

I felt the same way a few weeks later when a dinner was given for all the workers. Everybody got up to tell how they had become involved, and more than half of them said they were there because of me. I felt privileged to know that so many good people had dedicated themselves to a cause that was so necessary to the goals of diabetes education and research.

The team of more than fifty volunteers started working in April for the event in September. The group was especially fortunate to have the talented help and support of the Neiman-Marcus staff. Their expertise and knowledge – and a concern for the operation and image of the store – were brought to bear on every detail of our planning. For example, the store requested that we use *only* linen napkins and crystal glasses!

Believe me, it was a very big, very complicated job to put on an elegant and exciting event in a department store. Although it was the first such event in the Beverly Hills store, the Neiman-Marcus staff drew on their experience in putting on similar events in other stores, and they had all the logistics worked out. (*See Page 70*)

The Neiman-Marcus staff handled so many of the details that we were free to concentrate on areas of additional fundraising, such as the preparation of the Souvenir Journal that was given to all participants in the Caper. The advertising was a good source of revenue, and the Souvenir Journal also included an informational and instructional manual for the Treasure Hunt itself.

The invitations, which requested black-tie attire, showed a maze in black-and-white with red and gold arrows in relief on slick white paper. The event was billed as "an event to remember," and it truly was – the Caper was designed to have it all.

The members, along with the Neiman-Marcus staff, were at the door to greet the guests who had left their cars with the valet service. Cocktails were served at 6:30 p.m., and the Treasure Hunt began at 7:00 p.m. By eight o'clock, the participants were invited to dine at a continuous buffet and to join in the dancing. The food tables were set up on each of the four floors of the store, and each floor had its own special floral arrangements by different florists.

The real fun, of course, was to figure out the clues and follow the trail to one of more than 100 prizes, including a $2000 Bill Blass gift certificate, a weekend at the Beverly Hills Hotel, a trip to St. Croix (including a seven-day cruise in the Caribbean), Hartman luggage, Lady Godiva chocolates, Ferragamo shoes, St. John dresses, Ralph Lauren shirts, and on and on – a list of wondrous gifts.

As I stood at the top of the escalator and looked down at the glittering lights and beautifully dressed people, my feelings of pride and fulfillment really overwhelmed me. No one, but no one, could pay me enough money to buy the gratification that I felt at that moment. It was wonderful!

And it was a great relief when the evening was successfully concluded. I felt validated by the overflow crowd and the hard work of the volunteers. The truth is that I had been worried about the outcome. I am never complacent about fundraising projects, no matter how many times I work on them. There is always a part of me that reacts like it's my first event. It's normal to feel apprehensive until it's over, even though you know that everyone is doing their job.

That's what keeps you on your toes and enables you to sense problems in advance.

It was over! The Caper had fulfilled our greatest expectations by bringing in new leadership, recruiting more volunteers, raising money. A new audience was alerted to the complications of diabetes and the importance of finding a cure. And more than $110,000 was raised for diabetes research and education.

The committee has a group of hard working and caring volunteers. Each year they have continued to create unusual events that successfully raise money for this cause.

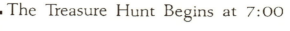

The Treasure Hunt Begins at 7:00

Welcome to the
GREAT CATALOGUE CAPER: "AN EVENING TO TREASURE."

You've just received a clue card similar to the one below. Embedded in the message is a valuable hint, one that leads you to unlock and locate over 100 treasures.

FOR EXAMPLE:
"He thinks he's the big cheese on this film, but he only smells like one."

ANSWER:
Epicure Department
A look at the clue card will lead you to the first of eighteen Treasure Chests located in Departments on all four levels of the store. This is where you will obtain additional clues that will help you unlock the mystery hunt to win one of the treasures.

If you are lucky enough to solve this clue just watch what happens.

Upon arriving at each Treasure Chest, one of our Neiman-Marcus Caper Captains will trade you a new clue for the one you just solved or perhaps you will draw a winning clue that will lead you immediately to The Winner's Circle on Level Two.

A NOTE OF CAUTION: Our Neiman-Marcus Caper Captains cannot be bribed! They only have information pertaining to their respective locations.

The more clues you solve, the quicker you solve them, the greater your chances of winning fabulous treasures from Sea Goddess, Galanos, Baccarat, DIVA by Parfums Ungaro, Spago Restaurant, The Beverly Wilshire Hotel and MORE.

The mystery hunt will continue until all of the treasures have been won.

Any questions? Direct them to the Neiman-Marcus Caper Captain in the "Winner's Circle" on Level Two in the Couture Salon.

Good Luck and Happy Hunting!

Logistics – How to Play

ELEVEN

MONEY

"*There is an old saying: 'Money Makes the World Go Round,'* " *observes Annette.* "*Whether generally true or not, it certainly is the principal ingredient in making an organization work. Blended with dedicated leadership and hardworking volunteers, it is a component that raises the organization to new heights and promises continuing growth as well as needed money for the cause.*"

Annette smiles, shifts her position, takes a deep breath, and asks: "*Do people like to give money? How do you get people to give money? When? Where? How?*"

Although I know that money is important, it is also a most personal and intensely sensitive subject for almost everyone. I believe that each person can be motivated to give on a level that is appropriate for them. The challenge is to find out how.

Family problems, personal relationships and sex are talked about with frankness and honesty, but money is still a difficult subject. Almost any query about money can make a person tense and hostile.

Why? People who work at raising money have pondered and discussed this question for years. Psychological tests, in-depth studies, training sessions, and debates in both public and private settings have produced widely divergent answers and approaches – but money still remains a sacred cow.

Connect Money to the Cause

Even in casual gatherings where no money is actually being raised, comments about money will bring hostile reactions, and everyone seems to have a favorite horror story about being solicited for money.

Fundraising is the bottom line of many volunteer organizations and it's my strong point as a professional volunteer. It has the elements that excite, challenge and motivate me. I'm concerned about doing the best job possible for the organization I represent. I know when raising funds it is important to be prepared with information about the organization and be clear about its goals.

Suppose, for instance, I am at a dinner party or perhaps a sports event. I like people, and so I usually start a conversation. The other person may have heard that I am involved with a fundraising group and will mention it. That's just the lead I need to start talking about what the group is doing. If they seem interested, I may invite them to meet some other people or to participate in an upcoming meeting. I've had great things happen on just such a simple one-on-one contact.

But I will not mention money in the first conversation. I believe that if people know something about what a group is actually doing and accomplishing, it will be easier to approach them at the right time for a contribution. The secret is to know the right time!

The right time comes when you have provided an opportunity for people to make a contribution in a setting where they feel comfortable. How? Many groups will sponsor an event that requires an initial donation – a premiere, a luncheon, a dinner, an ad book. All of these activities provide a financial baseline, and offer a clue to the potential donor as to the range of appropriate gifts. Then, too, the event itself gives something back to the contributor, allows the contributor to feel good about her or his gift, and gives a feeling of being in command.

Enjoy the Experience

I really believe you should have fun when you are raising or giving money. Although the making of a financial contribution is a very serious and important decision, it is also a way for people to get together and support a good cause while having a good time. The more positive the experience for the new donor, the more successful the event will be – and the more likely it is that the first-time donor will become more involved in the organization. I've discovered that people who continue to support an event year after year tend to become more and more happily involved, and then the amount of their gift increases.

It's always necessary to make people understand why their gifts are so important. For example, I wonder if people realize that government support for many causes takes into account the number of private donors and the amount of money that an organization is able to raise on its own?

When an agency is considering a request for government funding, the officials will many times look at computer print-outs to see how much money the organization is able to raise on its own, and they assess the level of public interest and support for a particular cause. Then a decision is made about providing government dollars through allocations and grants. An organization with a healthy base of supporters will find it easier to convince the decision-makers in government that their programs are important to the community and worthy of support. This is another vital reason for supporting a cause that is significant to you, and it's a way of motivating others to understand the importance of their giving.

What's Right?

Of course, it also helps if you are working with a group that is knowledgeable and interested in the cause. That's when your words can give them a good reason for maximum giving.

For example, I was recently asked to be the solicitor and speaker in Seattle for a women's fundraising event that benefits the United Jewish Appeal. The minimum donation was $5000, and the women who were invited to the event knew in advance the amount of the donation that is required.

The leadership of the Seattle community included some familiar faces. I had been one of the motivators who worked with members of the Seattle Women's Division when the group came to Los Angeles on a tour of places of Jewish interest several years earlier.

The work that I did with the Seattle delegation is part of my responsibilities as a member of the Board of Directors of the National Women's Division of the United Jewish Appeal. The National Women's Division includes women from all over the United States who are given the responsibility of programming, training and solicitation in various areas of the country.

One of my assignments is to serve as a Community Consultant. I truly enjoy visiting the communities around the country, meeting women who share the same concerns of comunity and Israel. I have been involved as a Community Consultant with Women's Divisions in Orange County, Long Beach, Santa Barbara, Palm Springs, and Seattle.

When the Seattle group came to Los Angeles, their organization needed a defining purpose. Traveling and studying as a group, seeing the thriving Jewish community in Los Angeles, gave new impetus and excitement to the organization and its leadership. When the women left Los Angeles, they were infused with a new spirit and a new level of enthusiasm for their work. Although many years have passed since that visit, they still feel that the visit to Los Angeles was a turning point.

Special Challenges

Now it was my turn to travel to Seattle on behalf of the United Jewish Fund. The event posed some special challenges. The minimum donation was sizable. Of course, at that level of giving, I knew that I would be meeting with interested and knowledgeable women. But I also knew that their expectations of a speaker would be high.

Before my trip to Seattle, I made sure that I understood my assignment and the background of the people whom I would be addressing. It is very important to me to talk with people, not at them; that's what forges a partnership between the solicitor and the donor.

I knew that the commitment of these women was strong, but I always like to provide myself with extra insurance. I did it by giving the leadership a personal gift – a book of quotations that I have always found inspirational. Somehow, I find that such a gesture warms up the audience, and when we share something that I care about, I become a part of the group.

I met with the committee in Seattle on the evening before the event, and they were concerned about how I would raise funds. Their concern translated to: Would I be assertive and demanding? Would I pick out certain people to ask for their contribution? How would I raise the maximum dollars and still keep everybody happy and feeling comfortable about their contributions?

They suggested an outline of my remarks. This proves once again that a fundraiser can never be complacent; you always have to prove yourself. I assured them that I was a low-key fundraiser, and no one would be pressured or made to feel uncomfortable. But they would have to trust me.

Preparation of a speech is the key

I had prepared my talk carefully in order to make the necessary points and elicit the appropriate reaction from the audience. In preparing myself, I was aware that it is always important to give people the opportunity to respond with their own experiences, to relate their personal concerns and special interests, and to identify their family backgrounds.

When I arrived at the home where the luncheon and meeting was to be held, I was pleased at the beautiful room with its lovely setting and an audience of gracious and happy people. Just the way I like it! Everyone seemed delighted to be a part of such a gathering.

It is important for a speaker to check out the room to make sure the physical set-up is good. For example, never stand in front of a picture window with a fascinating view, or any other background that may detract from your message! And don't be afraid to change the setting if it's not appropriate for you.

A speaker must realize that only seven percent of the message comes across in the words that are actually spoken. Thirty-eight percent comes across in your voice: strong or weak, loud or soft, tense or relaxed. Fifty-five percent comes across in your facial expressions and reactions as you speak. What this adds up to is the fact that ninety-three percent of your talk is non-verbal.

Thus, it is important for every speaker to be aware of attitudes, feelings, inflection, and appearance as well as the words themselves. That's the only way to reach out to an audience for a positive reaction. A speaker is a conductor who must know all the notes in order to make the music blend while highlighting and synchronizing all the instruments and bringing the performance to a harmonious and dramatic conclusion.

That is why I try to be conservative in the way I appear before an audience, including the choice of clothes, jewelry and make-up. I don't want somebody to be so curious about something I'm wearing that they forget to listen to what I am saying.

Introduction of a talk

The introduction is a pertinent part of getting to know the background of the speaker. In my various roles this has been an important part of setting the stage. Many speakers send pages of personal information and this is not always practical to use. If a speaker wants a specific introduction, it is advisable that the chairman is contacted before the event and given a script.

While I sat waiting to speak at the Seattle event, I realized that the music stand where I would put my notes was too low. After the introduction, as I stepped up in front of the audience, I raised the stand and made a comment about how on many occasions my height has put me in funny situations. That little gesture relaxed me, and I began to speak.

I thanked everyone, took a deep breath, waited for everyone to quiet down, and observed that the lovely room was filled with women of all ages – mothers, daughters, friends. I felt that my approach would work.

The talk went well. They were listening. This revealed their interest and stimulated personal reponses. The first response came from a women I knew. Then I relaxed because I knew that my approach was working. For more than forty-five minutes, the women followed each other in their eagerness to speak about their own feelings, their own experiences, and their desire to make a contribution. It was a catharsis and, more important, a successful fundraiser.

After my talk, many women came up and thanked me for the opportunity to share their feelings and experiences. They also expressed the good feelings they had about understanding each other and the role they played in the day's success.

Then it was time to leave. Only twenty-four hours or so had passed since I left home, but I was fulfilled by the challenges of those few hours. Needless to say, when a meeting is successful, I am excited, motivated and ready for the next challenge. Raising money is an accomplishment and a real high for me.

Money may be the most difficult word to deal with, but always remember that it's a five-letter word that makes things happen!

TWELVE

POWER

Life begins at birth, and so does the pursuit of power. A baby asserts itself with its cry for attention. And so we continue through life, measuring and testing our power in each encounter and experience, exerting our strengths to an ever-changing audience. Whether we are aware of it or not, life is a struggle for power.

"I hate the word," says Annette. "It bothers me that power and money seem to go together. Too often, people with only material assets are given preference. I can't explain what bothers me, but I believe by doing things in a dignified manner you earn respect. Power does not give a person dignity."

The Definition of Power

The dictionary defines the word power as the ability to act or produce, to act strongly, to control others, or a special authority assigned to or exercised by a person holding an office.

I accept the value of power when a person has a position of responsibility – an office in government or an organization –

and it is important for him or her to accomplish his or her stated goals. Such a person has a mandate to use the power of the office in order to discharge the duties to the group.

If a person takes a job and doesn't do anything with it, then the power of the position is wasted. One must also understand that power must be exercised wisely and with tact and discretion. The person who wields power must act with sensitivity and understanding; he or she should not take advantage of the power and authority that comes with an office or position.

Unfortunately, there are many people who use their power arbitrarily to forward their own opinions without providing a forum for further discussion. Some people are tempted to demonstrate how powerful they are by abusing others through inconsiderate and insensitive actions. Wielding power at the expense of others is the behavior of an immature person who hasn't gotten over the "me" feeling. When I see this kind of abuse of power, my opinion of the person drops; it's a sure sign that the group is in trouble, and that is sad.

There is another facet of this: it is the persons who won't let go of their power or position. This, too, can be destructive and dangerous. The refusal of leaders of longstanding to make room for new faces will stymie the growth of the organization and ultimately lead to its downfall. New people bring in fresh ideas and different perspectives.

The misconception or misuse of power can make or break a person or an organization. The danger signals are unmistakable: decision-making is narrowed to a very small contingent or even a single person, attendance declines, membership drops off, recruitment diminishes, meetings are limited in scope, and debate is curtailed. People will look for more democratic organizations with more opportunities for participation as well as a platform for their views to be heard and considered.

Although I'm still not comfortable with the word "power," or the connection between money and power, I believe it does not necessarily mean that one has to have money to have power. Sometimes power may be acquired by hard work, dedication, and the development of contacts. And even when money gives you a platform to make your views known, it's still up to you to know what you are going to say, what you want to accomplish, and how to accomplish it.

The Power of the Platform

Careful preparation will help you make the best use of the "power of the platform," and that is another way to exercise influence within an organization. When I make a presentation – whether it's a brief proposal, a training session, a keynote speech, or a fundraising solicitation – I prepare my remarks carefully. I research the facts, study the pertinent materials, assemble the necessary information, and only then do I put words to paper.

Doing my homework gives me the power to control or at least influence the audience for a given amount of time during my presentation.

I always make a point of knowing in advance whom I will be addressing – the age, background and sex of the group – as well as the time of day, the place, and the size of the audience. The more you know about your audience, the better prepared you will be. Of course, it is essential to keep in mind the purpose of the talk – fundraising, education, training, or information. While this may seem basic, the fact is that many speakers take assignments without knowing the true focus of the group or the appropriate focus of the speech. If you've ever attended an event where the audience is disoriented by the speaker, you can appreciate the importance of these fundamentals.

I consider it a privilege to be invited to speak to an organization. I am always aware of my responsibility to my audience. I realize being a speaker can be an important position of power if used respectfully. I want to do the best job possible.

The request for me to speak usually comes by telephone, and so I am given the basics: time, place, group, length of talk, theme, purpose of meeting. I ask for the call to be followed up by a written confirmation. However, if I have further questions, I do not hesitate to call the group to get the answers.

Once I've accepted the assignment, I begin to think about what I want to say. I am a great collector of quotes and brochures that cover many different subjects. I also count on current news to give me clues on what is timely. I make a point of putting in some personal anecdotes; people like to know something about the speaker that isn't included in the customary introduction or biographical information. And I make sure that my facts are correct, especially when I cite statistics or use quotes; always count on someone in your audience to be as knowledgeable as you, and if the facts are incorrect, you will lose your credibility.

Once I know the basics, I formulate a goal and a theme for my talk. Then I outline my subject, and start filling in the details. This approach allows me to organize and develop the material that I have assembled while keeping the purpose of my talk in mind. Be sure you are comfortable with your material; be sure that you can present your ideas and information with sincerity and conviction. Don't underestimate the importance of your own motivation in delivering an honest and earnest talk.

Once I have everything pulled together, I am ready to write my speech on five-by-seven file cards. The file cards make it easy for me to refer to my notes without getting lost in the middle of a page, and allow me to interchange material that will be relevant in other talks. Since I give many presentations a year, it is helpful for me to use well-researched material for different audiences. This includes introduction, presentation, preparing agendas for conducting meetings, and any other discussions when I need to have my facts accurate. Sometimes I will use manuscript pages and use a brightly-colored pencil to underline the passages that I want to emphasize.

Respect for Your Audience

I can't stress enough the importance of having respect for your audience. You never know how informed your audience is; also, assume they are interested and involved people who are there to learn. They expect to hear something special from you. Never talk down to an audience. They can tell the difference between a phony and a sincere speaker within minutes of your first words.

It's also important to maintain as much eye contact as possible with the audience. Reading a speech is acceptable if you are a good reader, and referring to notes is appropriate, but you must always remember to look at your audience as often as possible.

Never apologize if you are late or have a problem. You are there to give a talk; give it. Nothing is more annoying to an audience than listening to a speaker go on for several boring minutes explaining his or her shortcomings; the speaker is stealing valuable time from an audience that came to hear a talk. Never use the audience as a punching bag for your insecurities and all the world's ills. As a speaker, you have the power and the opportunity to put your ideas across. You are in control. Use the power!

The Power of Vision

As a leader we can demonstrate trust, hope and vision. Without vision there is no future. This is a declaration that made me realize the importance of organizing the Women's Committee and the Women, Power and Money Forum of the Jewish Community Foundation

As women, we recognize that we have a special role to provide for our children, grandchildren and beyond and to ensure a healthy and secure Jewish community in which to participate and thrive. To accomplish this goal, we will have to provide for the future needs of our Jewish community in Los Angeles and Israel.

The Jewish Community Foundation's various endowment programs provide a unique opportunity to enable us to achieve our goals. Through the Women's Foundation Committee and the Jewish Community Foundation we will seek to:

- Inform and educate about the Foundation, charitable giving, estate planning and changing community needs.
- Motivate and generate future involvements in the Women's Foundation Committee and the projects and programs of he Jewish Community Foundation, such as the endowment of a woman's United Jewish Fund Annual gift.
- Understand and utililize the financial power and decision making ability that women have.
- Create goodwill on the part of the Women's Foundation Committee and the Jewish Community Foundation.
- Create awareness and name recognition.
- Develop alternative endowment funding sources.

This has brought about some significant research which we must translate into needed dollars for service if we are to meet our expanding commitments.

It is necessary for us as women to look at and evaluate our estate planning no matter how large or small. We must educate ourselves as to how much we can and will contribute to future generations.

Power is a five-letter word. Power is a partner to money, but it is much more. Power is a tool to influence people. It is a co-worker with knowledge and learning. It is dedication and constant activity. It is the life force that gets things done.

THIRTEEN

MILESTONES

W*e cannot tell what may happen to us in the strange med-
ley of life. But we can decide how to cope with whatever hap-
pens to us. That is what really counts in the end. How to take
the raw stuff of life and make it a thing of worth and beauty –
that is the test of living.*

"I have been especially privileged to experience many
wonderful and significant events over the years," Annette
observes in a moment of reflection. "Some have been sad
and scary, some have been joyous and beautiful. All of them
represent the milestones and stepping stones in my life."

Israel

The birth of the State of Israel in the spring of 1948, for
example, coincided with the marriage of Annette and
Leonard Shapiro, and the family has been deeply influenced
by events in the Jewish homeland.

"Our children's generation has been honored to be the
first generation in 2000 years that can look to a Jewish state
in the land of our heritage," Annette explains. "We have a
large family in Israel, and we have been there many times."

The family's first trip to Israel was in 1966 on the occasion of Joel's Bar Mitzvah. This was a time of reunion with Leonard's family who had immigrated to Israel in the 20's and 30's. The many uncles, aunts and cousins embraced us with love and affection.

Leonard and Annette have returned on numerous study missions and as representatives of the Los Angeles Jewish community for the United Jewish Fund. "I look forward to my trips to Israel with joy and excitement," says Annette.

"I remember just such anticipation when my cousin Sandy and her daughter Debra (still in high school) decided to make their first visit to Israel on a Women's Mission. At first I hadn't planned to go but the more I thought about them going on their first trip, the more excited I became. Finally, during a dinner party, I made a decision. I phoned Sandy right then. When she answered, I said: I'm going to Israel, too. I couldn't let you go on your first trip there without being with you to share such a wonderful experience."

In 1973, however, the visit was a sad one. Annette was invited to participate in a special leadership mission following the Yom Kippur War in her capacity as Women's Division Chairman for the Greater Los Angeles United Jewish Fund.

"It was a sorrowful, heartbreaking visit as we went from hospital ward to hospital ward talking with the young soldiers," Annette recalls. "They were so terribly wounded, some without arms or legs. One young man, badly burned, asked me to kiss him. 'No one would want to,' he said. I did. He was so young and hurting so much – my heart ached for him and the families who had suffered along with their sons. Many had come out of the ashes of the Nazi camps. Many had lost fathers in the earlier wars, and now the sons in this war. That's why the Yom Kippur War became known as the War of the Sons."

Annette's own family suffered a loss in war. Her cousin, Eric Regev was a paratrooper who was killed after the 1967 war. His widow, Ilana, watched their son Sharon follow in his path and serve as a paratrooper in the 1973 war.

The Shapiros visited Ilana's home in the Ramat Gan suburb of Tel Aviv, a section still called "the paratroopers neighborhood." In the living room was a photograph of Eric as a young, handsome soldier, and pictures of Eric and Ilana with their children.

Sharon had graduated from veterinary medical school in Romania; the Shapiros helped support his studies there. His laboratory was constructed in the garage of his mother's home. His two sisters lived at home, but Sharon and his bride live a few blocks away.

Family, Friends, Community

Trips to Israel throughout the years have enabled the Shapiros to keep in touch with family, friends, and the larger Jewish community. The study missions, Annette explains, bring together Jewish leaders from all over the world. Special visiting scholars share their knowledge and expertise with visiting community leaders, and one of these scholars – Holocaust survivor Gerda Klein – is a friend of Annette's.

Among the other notables with whom Annette became acquainted were Valerie and Galina Panov, the Russian ballet stars who Annette met soon after their release from the Soviet Union. "They were thankful to world Jewry which persisted and worked so hard to get their release," Annette recalls. "They said, 'People have written letters, talked to the government, and given money; they have done so much for our release. Will we be good enough to have made it worthwhile?' Those of us fortunate enough to have seen them dance know they were 'good enough.' "

Annette also encountered less glamorous but no less noble and endearing men and women throughout Israel. The study missions include visits to agencies and centers where services are provided to the citizens of Israel. On one such visit to a Nutrition Center that provides meals for senior citizens, Annette met an elderly gentlemen.

"Share with me a sandwich of love," he said, gallantly handing her a slice of rye bread and butter. Says Annette: "It was the most delicious sandwich I have ever eaten."

Europe…and Again Israel

Travels have taken Annette and Leonard to many exciting and interesting places throughout the world. A special interest of theirs has always been visiting Jewish communities wherever they are. On a UJA mission to Poland and Romania, Annette stood in the snow at Auschwitz, the notorious death camp in Poland. "I felt so cold and afraid," she remembers. "Ghosts were all around. We walked into an empty barrack and I really believed I could hear cries in the stillness. I felt despair in the empty room. Piercing the quiet was the lonely sound of a train whistle. Thank God it brought me out of the horrible past to the present…."

In contrast, the next stop was Bucharest, Romania, at which time she shared a special lunch with members of the aged Jewish community there. At this lunch, they served cornmeal mush, which was so reminiscent of her childhood as this was a weekly dish her grandmother had made on visits to her home when Annette was growing up.

While in Bucharest at the retirement home, "I felt love and affection as a lady grasped my hand and said: 'You look so much like my daughter (who died years ago.) Thank you for not forgetting us.' " The following day the mission was on the flight to Israel.

"Israel", Annette explains, "always brings me the anticipation of renewal. In Israel, nothing is ordinary. Coincidences become striking stories. Greetings, meetings and reunions are all part of the mystique."

Annette has a special fondness for one such greeting. In 1971, she traveled to Israel on a Women's Mission. The members of the Mission had been alerted that a planeload of refugees from the Soviet Union was expected. Could they

With President Chaim Hertzog and his wife.

Annette and Leornard with Itzhak Shamir.

Ellie Weisel, our guest at a special University of Judaism event.

Jean Kirpatrick, former Representative in the United Nations, was guest speaker at United Jewish Fund event.

Dianne Feinstein, former San Francisco Mayor, now California Senator, pictured with Annette at a political fund-raising event at the Shapiro home.

IMPORTANT EVENTS

Joel Grey performs in concert at the University of Judaism

Madeleine Kunin, Governor of Vermont at a pre-lecture UJ reception at the Shapiro home.

Annette with Ron Ruron, former Israeli Consulate and Barbara McClusky at a women's meeting for support of Israel.

A proud moment; David's involvement in Diabetes activities gives Annette special pride.

From left: Dr. Patrick Soon Shiong. Kathryn Iacocca Hentz, Lee Iacocca, Annette and Leonard at the dedication of the Pancreas-Transplant and Diabetic Research Laboratory.

Annette, in Moscow, waits with Russian woman in long line for visa to Israel.

A Russian immigrant finds a new home in Israel.

Participants in a National Women's Division Mission had the privilege of welcoming Russian immigrants at the airport in Israel. It was a glorious moment for children as well as parents.

Ethiopians have been arriving in Israel for the past decade. This young girl will find her future "Israeli" a dream come true.

The Russians arrive in Los Angeles and meet their new family.

We are one. Welcoming new Russian family to our home.

Rosanne Keefer, 1980

The vibrant color of this flower,
Is an example of our volunteer power.
A beautiful rose with its color so bright,
As a volunteer, we try to make lives right.
My volunteer career started like a rosebud,
And has turned out to be my own life's blood.

— Annette Shapiro

be ready within minutes after the call came, no matter what time of day or night? More than 150 women shouted in unison: "Yes!"

As it happened, the women were just finishing dinner when the call came. They took the flower arrangements from the dinner tables, boarded the buses, and arrived at the airport in time to greet the big plane. "We had planned to sing as the newly-arrived refugees walked from the plane," Annette recalls, "but as the door opened and the first person appeared, our voices choked...*and that man seemed to me to be my own grandfather of blessed memory.*"

The women from America greeted their sisters and brothers from the Soviet Union in the reception area. "Some of the refugees could speak English, and – miracle on miracle – one young woman had relatives in our own neighborhood back in California," says Annette. "Months later, the young woman came to visit her family, and we all had a wonderful reunion."

A Woman Named Golda

The high point of the mission, Annette recalls, was an audience with Golda Meir, then serving as Prime Minister of Israel.

"It was on the last day of our visit, and rumors about a meeting with the Prime Minister had been flying – yes, we would; no, we wouldn't. We were all on a high with anticipation. Then the news – it was a go! We got all dressed up in the outfits brought especially for such an occasion. The guides who had seen us through the past week in jeans, sweatsuits and tennis shoes marveled at the effect one woman could have on so many others."

The memory of that exciting day has never left Annette. "I'll never forget it. We all had to have our badges in plain sight, and we were directed to a special room for inspection. The meeting was held at the Jewish agency in a council chamber. The room was filled with people."

"Then Golda Meir entered the room. Golda greeted us warmly, and there was so much good feeling between us. I'll never forget her first question, which seemed directed just to me: 'How many of you have been to Israel before?' I was so proud to say I had."

The Golda Meir Award

A parallel to that wonderful moment came many years later. On a glorious June day in Beverly Hills, the women dressed so very fashionably in their colorful spring outfits added to the Monet landscape of green lawns, blue pool, multicolored flowers, and bright umbrellas.

This was the setting for the Awards and Installation event of the Women's Division of the United Jewish Fund of Greater Los Angeles. The coveted Golda Meir Award for Outstanding Community Leadership was to be awarded to Annette.

Although she has received numerous awards for her myriad activities, this latest honor reflected her own deep respect and admiration for Golda Meir. In her acceptance, Annette expressed a feeling of awe for the Great Lady of Israel. She also explained that she was going to make a most specific visit to Israel.

Annette and Leonard were leading a family mission for the United Jewish Appeal, an international organization, and they were bringing their own grandchildren, Ben and Erin. A highlight of the trip would take place in the ancient synagogue on Masada, where Annette and Erin would each celebrate a symbolic Bat Mitzvah.

Annette has continued with her interest in the Jewish Federation Council and the United Jewish Fund for almost four decades. She continues to serve where she is needed, locally, nationally and internationally. It is a committment and a confirmation of her service to others.

Earlier Milestones

Another milestone was Annette's first opportunity to join

in the work of the Foundation for the Junior Blind in the early 1960s. "Actually, it was Leonard who got me started," explains Annette. A friend had a son who was partially blind. He asked for a donation of some plumbing supplies. When Leonard went to the Foundation to check on the materials needed, he asked me to go with him."

The facility, Annette remembers, was located in an old building that had been used by a military school. Leonard and Annette were both impressed by the activities that were offered to the children, and the sensitivity and care with which they were treated by the staff. Then Leonard said to Annette: "Why don't you get involved? Your help is needed."

Annette suggested to the Valley Guild for Children that the organization make efforts to support the Foundation for the Junior Blind, and the subsequent fundraising programs were very successful. "We had a Christmas party for the children," says Annette. "We took them Christmas shopping, and on an outing to Disneyland. It was truly a beautiful experience."

At the time, David Shapiro was not yet diagnosed as a diabetic. "We had no idea that we would personally be touched by a disease that has serious complications that can affect the eyes," Annette points out. "David has experienced eye problems as a result of diabetes, but fortunately it has been corrected through proper treatment. At the Foundation, there are children who are blind or partially sighted as a result of the disease. I will always personally consider the Foundation an important agency in the community."

Recognition

Celebrate The Mirabella 1000

Mirabella is celebrating its fifth anniversary this June and we're planning a terrific milestone issue! We invite you to participate. The anniversary edition is devoted to one theme: the celebration of women-our personal heroes.

We invite you to look to your own personal heroes-women you admire for their talent, innovation or service to a community, organization or idea.

They may be women who, in ways great and small, instigate and inspire positive change.

You may wish to acknowledge them for their ability to challenge us to see the world and ourselves in positive new ways, thereby expanding our sense of possibilities. Or you may wish to recognize the work, discipline, self-sacrifice and personal risk we know their missions often demand.

When Sandy Smalley, Annette's cousin, read these words, she wrote a letter to Mirabella. The following are some excerpts from Sandy's two page single spaced letter:

"The Mirabella 1000, Annette Shapiro, one in a million!When I read about the Celebration of Women in the December 1993 issue of the *Mirabella* magazine, one name, Annette Shapiro, immediately came to my mind. Your description of women for whom you were looking fit Annette to a "T".

She is that woman who inspires others with her vision and activities which do so much to influence and illuminate the daily lives of others – truly a personal hero. These qualities along with her service to the community, organizations, and far reaching ideas perfectly describe Annette Shapiro.

While speaking of involvement, I could fill a book with her activities and awards, and I know that the enclosed information will speak for itself. You should also know that as of 1989 Annette decided that she wanted no more awards, as the satisfaction which she derived from her activities in helping others was more than adequate.

With all of Annette's personal responsibilities, among them her seven grandchildren, with whom she spends a great amount of time, she *alway* finds the time to listen and to help, on an individual level, someone who is in need. She is also the perennial hostess in her home for celebrations of her family and friends. In addition to these festivities, Annette and Leonard's lovely home is *always* open for an art tour of their contemporary art collection, a charity event, or a family gathering which sometimes numbers seventy five to a hundred relatives. It is never too much for her. She is the busiest person I know, and it is difficult to comprehend how she finds the time for it all. But she does it, and *always* with a smile and grace.

I hope that you have gotten to know Annette Shapiro, and am convinced that you will come to the same conclusion that I have. Annette deserves to be a part of the Mirabella Celebration.

Sincerely,
Sondra Smalley

This letter from the *Mirabella* editors followed:

Congratulations! You are listed in our special June 1994 issue as one of the 1,000 most influential women in America today. The issue celebrates Mirabella's 5th anniversary which highlights the progress and outstanding achievements of women today.

The Not So Pleasant

Some of Annette's memories of her volunteer work are not so rewarding. "I think it's important to mention them," she insists, "so others can be aware that there may be some negative experiences, too."

For example, when Annette served as Chairman of the Women's Division of the United Jewish Fund, the keynote speaker at a fundraising luncheon was Abba Eban, former Ambassador of Israel to the United States. The luncheon took place at a country club, and photographs were taken. A photograph of Abba Eban, Annette and another woman later appeared in the local newspaper.

"A few days later, the club received a letter with a copy of the newspaper photograph, and our faces were covered with swastikas," Annette says. "The unsigned note with the clipping said: 'We know where you are and we will get you.'

That was the strongest personal anti-Semitic attack I had ever experienced. When I read it, I began to cry. It was frightening."

Another situation, different in tone but equally frightening, took place in a very public setting at a meeting of the Los Angeles County Board of Supervisors. "I was there to speak in favor of animal research to find a cure for diabetes and other catastrophic diseases," Annette says. "Tests conducted on pound animals and animals raised specifically for research are important and have yielded dramatic results."

Annette attended the meeting with a friend who is alive and well today because of the medical advances that resulted from such research. "A man behind us kept hissing and calling us evil. It was very frightening to realize that such fanaticism exists. The hatred of this person was so strong we feared he might do something desperate; he didn't care about us or our feelings or our cause. It proves again that even good and necessary causes have their intolerant persons who have to be fought."

FOURTEEN

THANK YOU

If you have hard work to do
Do it now
If you have a song to sing
Sing it now
If you have kind words to say
Say them now
Do a kindness while you may
Loved ones will not always stay
Say them now
If you have a smile to show
Show it now
Make hearts happy, roses grow
Let the friends around you know
The love you have before you go
Show it now

"For me, giving is a way of saying 'Thank you' for the opportunity to live and work in this wonderful world," Annette explains thoughtfully as she focuses her attention on the family photographs arranged in a variety of attractive frames on the grand piano.

The living room has been designed for comfort and entertainment. Its contemporary styling creates the perfect backdrop for the extraordinary display of abstract art. The artwork has been blended to create a feeling of excitement.

Two large glass coffee tables display the Shapiro family's interest in arts and travel with beautifully bound books and scrapbooks. An especially handsome scrapbook, bound in red leather and embellished with gold markings, displays photographs of a trip to China with Bernard Shapiro (Leonard's brother) and his wife, Rena, in October 1985.

Rena, known as "Renny" to her friends and family, recalls the trip to China with pleasure. "It was great fun and went so well," Renny says. "We had some misgivings about all four of us being on the same airplane – Bernie and Leonard are both officers of the Familian Company – and it was such a foggy, misty night that we were glad the people who hold our insurance couldn't see us all together."

Renny met Annette when she was fourteen years old and started dating Bernard. "I've always admired her greatly, and our relationship has been one of mutual respect and affection, a close family relationship," Renny explains. "Bernie's Mom established the family's strong ties. I don't think anyone would have dared to behave otherwise. So none of us would ever allow anything to disrupt our family relationships. The brothers have opposite personalities, but both of them have an abiding family loyalty."

Annette's qualities, according to Renny, include directness and self confidence. "When she gets up to speak, her honesty and sincerity come right from the heart," says Renny. "She talks as if she had been trained at the finest university. Her self-assurance takes over in situations that call for an expert. She is the first one to ask questions when she doesn't know something. When she hears the correct procedure, she moves ahead with solving the problem."

Renny recalls how her children regarded their "Auntie" Annette. "My kids looked at her as an 'Auntie Mame,' " she says. "Annette was flamboyant and bursting with energy. Everything she did was on a grand scale, and she had an expansive personality. She gave off a quality of excitement and purpose. The nieces and nephews grew up having a feeling of Annette as a power figure rushing in and out, accomplishing great things. They still feel awed by her, and I think it matters very much what she thinks about them. They like to please her. They like to know that she approves of them."

The Shapiro Home

"To digress," Annette begins again, "I love this house. It's beautiful and wonderful, and I've tried to make it comfortable for us. It's me."

With large picture windows opening on the terrace, and wide green lawns encircling the blue pool, the living room has the feeling of an extended garden. The scene is sheltered with shade trees, including a 75-year-old Cooper beech.

"This room has provided a platform for many prestigious people who have spoken here on the arts, politics, health, welfare, and fundraising," Annette recalls.

The grounds include a rose garden, and that's one of the things that prompted Annette and Leonard to buy the house. "My father had a rose garden, too," Annette explains. "Roses are my own form of personal expression. I always bring flowers in a vase that I have selected for a particular person. Then I select the roses from my own garden. It gives me a good feeling, and it's one of the ways that I say 'Thank You.' "

Annette's gifts of roses is one of the gestures that her friends remember and appreciate. "When I was sick and didn't want to see anyone," one friend says, "there was a gift from Annette, a vase of roses. She came everyday to replace the roses with fresh ones."

Says Renny: "Annette has an intense loyalty to her old and dear friends. Some may not have moved along socially or financially, but she has never dropped these friends. Instead, she has admired and treasured the unique qualities in them that made them important to her through the years."

Another friend recalls how Annette came to their assistance when a fire destroyed their home. "When we got to the motel where we were staying," the friend says, "there was a gift from Annette. It was an address book and a calendar with a note: 'You gotta get organized!' "

Annette's gifts are known on an international scale. One of her mementos is a letter from the mother of Israeli actress Aviva Marks after Annette sent her a collection of clippings about her daughter:

"Today I received the pictures and write-ups and cuttings, and I cannot thank you enough. So thoughtful, so kind, and I am sure you know what it all means to a Mother to get such lovely reports. I expect my daughter told you that I am a widow and live alone. So when I get such a wonderful parcel as you sent me today, my feelings go beyond words. I simply broke down and howled my eyes out, not with sorrow but with great pride in her."

Hospitality

The Shapiro home has been the scene of many social gatherings. "I like to open my home to groups," Annette says. "I understand the need for people to get together."

Annette approaches the challenge of opening her home to fundraising events with the same commitment that characterizes her other volunteer work. "I feel very strongly that people who take on chairmanships for these events should know about the cause they are supporting," she says.

As an example, Annette recalls opening her home to a cocktail party for a group of 250 people to raise money for diabetes research and treatment. "When I met the chairperson, I asked her if she knew anything about diabetes. She said, 'Not really.' I said, 'As a parent of a diabetic I truly appreciate your efforts for this cause and I would like you to understand why. I will have a packet of information ready for you to read.' And I did. The material was in the mail to her the next day."

Another "opening" which was really fun also fulfilled a long time fantasy and concerned the guided bus tours that take sightseers through Beverly Hills. "I always had the desire to stop people who were on the tours and invite them into my home," Annette said. "Well, I finally got the chance and it really gave me such a kick. I had just returned from shopping and was bringing my packages into the house when I saw this group taking a walking tour. So I just asked the guide if the group would like to tour my home...Well, there was an immediate 'Yes' so they came through and oohed and aahed...they were very nice and later I received a thank you note from the Beverly Hills Chamber of Commerce asking if I would like to do this regularly."

The University of Judaism

Annette is especially proud of her work for the University of Judaism. She and Leonard are chairman of the school's continuing education program. The Department of Continuing Education(DCE) offers a wide variety of cours-es and study programs in Bible, Hebrew, Jewish history and contemporary life, Jewish living, women's studies, Jewish spirituality, as well as learning ventures in the arts – music, dance, drama, painting and sculpture.

Over 10,000 adult students a year attend the classes, the lectures, the Institutes, Study Tours, live-in experiences such as the University's famed Elderhostel program. "It is an outstanding community education undertaking", says Annette, "and what I really consider great about it is that no one pattern of thought or action is considered to be the only way to live and learn."

Of course, the base of the University's work is its undergraduate and graduate degree programs. These train students for future lay leadership in the Jewish and general communties – and rabbis, educators and communal workers for professional leadership in the Jewish world. "We feel privileged to be associated with this very consequential education venture – and adventure", Annette stresses.

The University of Judaism programs are open to participants of all ages, both on and off campus. "The idea of giving people the impetus to advance, to learn and explore new avenues of information through new methods is a wonderful challenge," says Annette. "As lay people interested in Jewish values and continuity, we find this a marvelous opportunity."

The Shapiro family found a unique way to support the University of Judaism and enhance its appeal to casual visitors to the campus. "I felt for a long time that there should be a gift shop of appropriate scale and style at the University of Judaism," says Annette. "The volunteers who work there have selected beautiful and unusual gifts to sell, but their facility was too small to properly display the lovely merchandise."

The solution was to design and build a new gift shop. "Leonard, the children and I joined with Renny, Bernie and their children in deciding that, as a tribute to the University of Judaism, we would make a major gift by endowing a gift shop. It's in the foyer of the administration building, and the simplicity of the glass-wall enclosure enhances the surroundings and brings out the beauty of the Jewish artifacts that are for sale, and the store is very successful."

Thank You

"Thank you can be said in many ways," Annette says. "It's not just a standard of leadership – it's something for all of us who have interchanges with other people. 'Thank you' are community words that belong to all of us. Everyone should use them more at any age, man or woman, boy or girl."

It's a lesson that Annette learned through her work as a volunteer. "I have a vivid recollection of one of the professionals I worked with because, after I chaired a meeting, there would always be a handwritten thank-you note."

Annette has learned that a thank-you is an important skill of leadership. "It takes so little time to say 'Thank you,' and the pleasure that it brings to the recipient is beyond monetary return," Annette explains. "Thoughtful actions do not need to be accompanied by a gift, a letter, or even immediate response; a telephone call of appreciation is also acceptable."

Annette continues: "If you have trouble saying 'Thank you,' try practicing before a mirror. The words come out easily without distorting the mouth or causing wrinkles. Think about the good feelings you have received from a brief note of appreciation, a simple thank-you, a friendly call, or a vase of fresh roses."

FIFTEEN

WHO AM I ?

Conversations with Annette were more and more hectic as she prepared for her next big project – the design and construction of a new family home. The old house had been sold, and the Shapiros were leaving for a European vacation before moving into a condominium where they lived while the new house was under construction. "Moving on, moving on," says Annette, "that's what life is all about." With boxes everywhere, phones ringing, doorbell chiming, and much scurrying around, it was a tumultuous scene.

"Who am I?" asks Annette Shapiro. "A wife? A mother? A daughter? A teacher? A sister? A leader? A friend? A student? A traveler? A volunteer?"

The answer, of course, is: all of these, and more.

How many roles have I played? So many beautiful, loving parts which have fulfilled me as a human being. Many of these roles are long-playing and continuous. Other roles have been played only in passing – the script and the action have changed. Many of the parts have been rewritten for different times, different places, and different audiences.

A Time to...

In all of these roles, I have found a time to build, a time to seek, a time to act, a time to pray, a time to change, and a time to choose. And whatever I have chosen to do, my goal was always to make things better. You might even call it a mission to make the world a more caring place.

In this quest for a better world, I have journeyed through many places and times. I recall the 1930s – the warmth and delicious smell of my grandmother's chicken soup, the discussions around my grandparents' dining room table, the heartbreaking news about what was happening in Germany, the crushing violence of World War II. I recall the 1940s – growing up in the San Fernando Valley, my parents showing me the importance of community service, commitment and involvement.

Each role brought new rewards. When I met Leonard, my roles expanded to wife and mother – glorious roles which brought new challenges and wondrous parts. More enrichment and love came with my role as a grandmother – real opportunities to perfect and validate my beliefs and ideals, an extension and renewal of the continuity of life.

Who am I? A woman who has had days and years of living, growing, learning, and loving. Times of sharing joys and sorrows. Looking ahead to years of doing and being.

I feel privileged to live in this time of historical firsts. As a witness to the past, I also represent the future. I go hand in hand with the generations. I feel an obligation to do my part – and I believe that through one's actions, lives change for the better.

I've felt especially fortunate to be a woman on the threshold of a new century. There have been great changes in my lifetime, but the greatest ones are still ahead. There are new frontiers that offer irresistible challenges.

Courage Is Everything

The family has faced the special challenge of David's deteriorating health and imminent surgery for a kidney implant. It was determined that Joel's kidney was a match, and we all felt a sense of relief – but also a new worry. Having my two sons in surgery at the same time caused tremendous fear and concern. No matter how strong you think you are, the worry is overwhelming and terrifying.

Personally and emotionally, I never thought I would ever get through those days. Then, the surgery was postponed for a month because of David's complication.

When the day of surgery actually arrived, I had the feeling: "Thank God it is here, and it's going to be over with soon." And, in fact, the surgery was over much faster than we anticipated.

It is really necessary for me to have hope and faith, and I truly do. There is going to be a cure for diabetes, and hopefully, David will be able to get that treatment. It is this belief that has driven me to do what I am doing. I will never stop working toward this goal.

Renny Shapiro served as chairman of the "Great Catalogue Caper," and she dedicated the evening to David and Joel. It came as a surprise when I heard her opening remarks, and it was very gratifying and encouraging.

David was the chairman of the Board of Directors of the Los Angeles Chapter of the American Diabetes Association. He was called to the podium to say a few words, and he asked Joel to come up with him. David greeted everyone, and then he described his gratitude to his brother and to his wife, Lynn, whose outstanding support and understanding were such a source of strength and comfort.

"1987 was a very difficult year for me and my family," David said. "I have had laser treatments, eye surgery, dialysis, and a successful kidney transplant. Because my brother Joel gave me one of his kidneys, I am not on dialysis any more. That was a wonderful gift of life."

David thanked everyone for attending the event, and for supporting diabetes research. "We hope to find a cure for diabetes," he concluded, "so other diabetics will not have to go through what I've been through!"

Seeing those two handsome, fabulous young men standing so tall and strong, I was a very proud and grateful mother. It would be difficult for anyone who had just met them to know what an ordeal they had just gone through. They both understand how important it is to tell their story; it will help others who must face the same challenges.

In order for their story to reach more people, David and Joel participated in a TV show called *Living Well With Diabetes* where they discussed their own experience of being brothers who were a recipient and donor of a kidney. This video has served as an inspiration to many people who are going through or contemplating this surgery.

Of all the wonderful things that happen in life, the best thing is good health. If you haven't got it, most other things pale in significance. That's why diabetes is such a difficult burden for both the people who suffer from the disease and their friends and family.

I am a private person in many ways, but I have never been private about my family's experience with diabetes. The only way we are going to find a cure for this disease is to talk out loud about it. The more people who talked about their own diabetic problems, the more others can relate to the disease. And when others realize the seriousness of diabetes and its life-threatening complications, we will have even more resources to help us find a cure.

"There Is No Getting Off"

In the early years, when I first started working for Diabetes, there was a great silence. No one wanted to talk about it. Now more people know about its devastating consequences, and that this desease is related to many other health problems. It is so important to bring diabetes to the attention of people, to help them understand the disease, so they will want to support diabetes causes.

Of course, it takes strength and courage to continue to be involved. I'm reminded of a situation that occurred at a meeting recently. It had been one of those days when everything in the world seemed off base – national disasters – political upheavals – community frustrations – and, to top it off, unseasonable "wet" weather, which makes most Californians miserable. About ten minutes into the meeting, a member got up and said: "I've had enough, I want to get off the train." I was shocked. Here was a devoted hard worker whose experience and advice were valuable to all of us. It was difficult for me to reconcile this casual decision with the seriousness of our work. I was angry! The victims of any catastrophic disease can't stop hurting. Their suffering continues! And so it is for other important causes that one is involved in. We must persist! Our journey is not completed until we reach our destination! Even if the ride is a rough one, there is no getting off!

People should never underestimate what they can accomplish; they will be constantly surprised by their own talents and capacities. Fear can stop you from accepting challenges, but my advice is: never let fear stop you. Go for it! That's the way to grow.

In all the years as a wife and mother, I've been involved and busy. It has enriched my life while allowing me to help other lives. The enthusiasm and excitement that I've been able to bring out in others has been great fun for me.

It's not a perfect world, and it was never meant to be, so we must accept the world as we find it – and then work hard to make it better. For example, we are building a new house. Do you think I'm not a little afraid? I am. And I know I'll make some mistakes. So what if it's not perfect? If I waited until everything was perfect, I would never accomplished anything.

We've lived for eighteen years in this house. We were here only a month when we had a big political rally for

600 people in the "backyard." Since then, it's been people and more people. I imagine that more than 10,000 people have been through this house. And, to bring it full circle, the Young Women's Division of the United Jewish Fund of Los Angeles will have a meeting here tomorrow.

I feel a little sad and nostalgic about saying goodbye to our house. But it's fitting to have a meeting here as a kind of ending of the era. My girls, Lisi and Lynn, will be here, too, which adds to the specialness of the day.

The chairwoman of the meeting asked me to be the speaker and talk about what being involved in the community has meant to me. I am always so pleased to explain the importance of volunteering and why it is so valuable to our individual growth. I know it will be a great morning!

SIXTEEN

CONTINUANCE – CHANGE – CHOICES

W*e are minutes, little things,*
Each one furnished with sixty wings.
We are but minutes, use us well
For how we are used we must someday tell;
Who uses minutes has hours to use,
Who loses minutes...whole years must lose.

Continuance and change

The act or process of continuing or lasting. The time during which an action, process or situation lasts.

The story of Annette Shapiro is a continuing one. The actions she takes are changes and choices and that is what makes her so enduring and special. "We are starting on a new phrase, a new area of our life, said Annette as she planned a new home and a 40th wedding anniversary. "Most important of all, we will have the joy of having our sons well again, and our family friends around us."

The anniversary celebration was unique and festive, and more than 350 of Leonard's and Annette's friends and relatives took part in the festivities: "Congratulations, continued good health, and best wishes to a wonderful couple" were the sentiments of the evening. The guests were given an opportunity to help tear down the old house on the site where the new Shapiro family home would be built.

The invitation was in rhyme:

> After 40 years we're still having a ball
> So we're celebrating this anniversary
> with an anniversary that will shake the walls.
> What a time! We'll dine, we'll dance around
> We'll live it up and tear the house down!
> For we're building a new home upon this site
> After the party Saturday night
> Your oldest jeans and tennies will be just fine
> Don't shop Rodeo – Try K-Mart this time.
> We look forward to sharing this night with you
> So come dressed as part of our "Wrecking Crew."

The guests included old and new friends – "How long have you known Annette and Leonard?" turned into a kind of party game. A proud reply of "Twenty years!" was met with a friendly scoff: "I was a bridesmaid at their wedding."

December 15, 1989: House completed

The house is finished! We feel the new Shapiro home combines the best of both architecture and interior decoration. It's a delightful place to live, and it adds a rewarding dimension to the Shapiro way of life.

The house is a marvelous showcase for the art collection which has been acquired on trips throughout the United States, Europe and the Orient.

Of course, there is a rose garden, which is perfect for the many occasions of entertainment .

There's a legend in Beverly Hills that Crescent Manor, the house which formerly occupied the site of the new Shapiro home, was built in 1910 by Florence Ziegfield. Debra Paget lived here. Mail for Ms. Paget is still being received!

The manor was one of the first residences in Beverly Hills, and the Shapiros were concerned that the 78-year-old structure would be designated as a historical landmark. When the Beverly Hills Planning Commission gave them the go-ahead, they were so excited that they could improve and update the property by building their own dream house!

In keeping with the Shapiro's "Open House" policy that was in effect in their other homes over the years, the "New Manor" has already been the scene of a political rally, a University of Judaism dinner and reception for Edgar Bronfman, President of the World Jewish Congress, an art tour for the Museum of Contemporary Art (MOCA) and the Los Angeles County Museum of Art, a gathering for the President of Israel, and a major fund-raiser for Diabetes honoring Lee Iaccoca and his daughter, Kathy.

A proclamation of the City of Beverly Hills, which was presented to Annette by Mayor Maxwell Salter, explains it well: Annette's home is "the top fundraising event location in Beverly Hills, moving just ahead of the Beverly Hills Hotel"!

Managing Change: The Challenge

Annette had some vigorous things to say about the phenomonen of change in our time. Let's listen...

The twenty-first century is less than a decade away. With so many possibilities in the future, I look forward to new projects to begin, new changes to encounter and experience. I am confident in my role, which is to accept and understand the changes. I count on it – and it's happening ever day. Changes fashion the goals of the future – new ideas, growth and continuance.

Change by definition is to pass from one phase to another. Change is what the world is all about. Change is what my world is all about.

Changes come about because of many events and influences, many of which we cannot control. How we handle these changes determines the future – and sometimes in unexpected ways. Many of the projects on which I've worked over the years have come full circle in ways that I could have never imagined.

In 1975, for example, a Soviet emigre named Galina Panov and I joined together in a candle-lighting ceremony in Los Angeles. Our purpose was to illuminate continuity, freedom and the right to live in peace and dignity anywhere in the world.

Today, Glasnost has changed the face of the former Soviet Union, as I witnessed for myself when I visited Russia as a passenger on the first El Al charter flight to Moscow. The privilege of freedom has been extended to thousands of Jews who are able to leave the land of their birth for the land of their choice. A candle flame has turned into a beacon of freedom.

As the light continues to glow, we have been able to locate my grandfather's family in Russia. This search was made possible throught the Jewish Family Service Immigration and Resettlement office. Our "newly" found cousins left Lvov, Russia and arrived in Los Angeles. We are delighted!

It was 1973 when I visited soldiers in hospitals in the aftermath of the Yom Kippur War. Now I feel a sense of excitement and fulfillment as I make plans to return to Israel as National Women's Division Co-Chairman of Missions to Israel. Now, more than ever, it is important to show our solidarity with Israel.

Whether it's Moscow or Israel or Los Angeles, there are always demanding and important needs in my world which I must be aware of all the time.

Making Choices

Choice implies an exercise of judgment in setting upon a course from among many offered, and choosing by careful discrimination from a large number of projects available.

About this Annette comments:

"I've had a lifetime of projects. They are a mystery until I get the clues – then it is up to me to make the right choices so that the project (mystery) can be solved or completed.

It's exciting and fun but a pressure activity that truly stimulates my thinking.

I look forward to the 21st century with so many possibilities, so many new choices. I have always been able to make choices, knowing that these would be reflected in the lives of my family and others around me. These choices have been in evidence throughout this book. They are reflected in the activities in my family, community, national and international. I believe strongly that as I've moved through the history of the past decades my choices have kept pace with the times.

I've been alert that a word, a gesture, an incident have an impact which may inevitably be the "change" reaction that moves us towards our choices. I am confident in my role which is to accept and understand the relationship between continuance, changes and choices. I am counting on it – because it is happening everyday. The goals of the future are ahead of me. I accept their... CHALLENGE."

Life has gone on for Annette Shapiro since the beginning of the writing of this book. She feels that she must move forward as a woman and as a professional volunteer. Her energy and creativity have sustained her while living a rich and full life. She continues to support all manner of causes, and she is still working in many organizations within the community and across the nation. Each day brings new experiences and new rewards to Annette Shapiro as a professional volunteer – a woman for whom continuance, changes and choices are a way of life.

EPILOGUE

When Annette and Leonard moved into their new home, the rose garden was a special part of their landscaping. I had the privilege of giving them a rose bush for their lovely garden. It is just now beginning to bloom – its name is First Edition!

A VOLUNTEER'S BIOGRAPHY

NATIONAL INSTITUTE OF HEALTH:

1985-87 National Diabetes Advisory Board of the National Institute of Health, Washington D.C. The responsibility of this board was to develop a National Long Range Plan to combat Diabetes.

Note: Mrs. Shapiro received this appointment in consideration of over 15 years of involvement with the Southern California Affiliate of the American Diabetic Association and service on the National Board of ADA

NATIONAL AMERICAN DIABETES ASSOCIATION:

1985-87 Nominating Committee

1986-88 Committee on Fundraising

1980-86 Board Member

1984-86 Committee Member of Task Force on Affiliate Program Development

Note: Mrs. Shapiro received the ADDISON B. SCOVILLE AWARD for Outstanding Affiliate Volunteer.

AMERICAN DIABETES ASSOCIATION SOUTHERN CALIFORNIA AFFILIATE:*

1992 Pre-Show Chairman-Premiere

1991-92 Liaison – Premiere/Caper/Caper

1976-87 Board of Directors

1977-87 Executive Committee

1988 Board Member

1981-83 Chairman of the Board

1977 Vice President

1977-79 Chairman-Premiere Committee**

Note: Today, Los Angeles is a Chapter of the American Diabetes Association, and California is an affiliate to the National Organization.

**Note: Mrs. Shapiro was very instrumental in the organization of the Premiere, which has been held for 19 successful years, raising in excess of $5 million.*

FOUNDATION FOR TRANSPLANT RESEARCH:

1992   Member of the Board

Both Mr. and Mrs. Shapiro are actively involved in support of Researcher and Surgeon, Dr. Patrick Soon-Shiong and his Diabetes Research Program. Dr. Soon-Shiong received FDA approval in 1992 for human clinical encapsulated islet cell transplants for a potential cure for Diabetes.

STOP CANCER:

1991-   Board of Directors

1992-   Vice President-Education

CITY OF HOPE:

1978   Testimonial Dinner given by the "Founders for the City of Hope" honoring Mrs. Shapiro. Purpose was to raise funds for the City of Hope. Large percentage of the funds raised supported the Diabetes Program. Monies raised: $420,000.

1978-88   Board of Trustees

1968-80   Member of Founders Club - Assisted in organizing "Founders for Diabetes Research"

1960-63   Vice President-Jr. Sportsmen

1954   Luncheon Chairman-Jr. Sportsmen Club

1946-48   Jr. Sportsmen Auxiliary of City of Hope

CEDARS SINAI MEDICAL CENTER:

1976-87   Committee Member for annual tennis tournament to raise funds for the Alfred J. Firestein Diabetes Unit

FOUNDATION FOR THE JUNIOR BLIND:

1977-88   Board of Directors

1977-80   Executive Committee

1966   President – Guild for Children

BETTY CLOONEY FOUNDATION FOR THE BRAIN INJURED:

1984-88   Board of Directors

1986   Committee-Annual Singers Salute to the Songwriters

JEWISH FEDERATION COUNCIL OF GREATER LOS ANGELES / THE UNITED JEWISH FUND/UNITED JEWISH APPEAL:

UJF is the fundraising arm of the Jewish Federation and raises money to support local Jewish needs and overseas needs for Jews throughout the world and in Israel.

Campaign Leadership: UNITED JEWISH FUND

1991   Co-Chair - $50,000 and over President's Council Event

1987-88   Campaign Co-Chair – $10,000 and over contribution dinner for UJF/Los Angeles

1974-76   Chairman – Women's Division UJF-Greater Los Angeles

1973-74   Co-Chair-Women's Division UJF-Greater Los Angeles

1970-71   Chairman- Women's Division, San Fernando Valley

1968   Inaugural Gifts Chairman, San Fernando Valley

1956   Co-Chair - Jr. Matron's Luncheon, San Fernando Valley

June 9, 1988 – Mrs. Shapiro was awarded the GOLDA MEIR AWARD for outstanding community leadership – Women's Conference, Jewish Federation Council of Greater Los Angeles.

Council Leadership:

The Jewish Federation Council is the organization that is representative of the programs and social services of the Los Angeles Community, Nationally and Worldwide.

1991-   United Jewish Fund Committee

1991-   Board Member

1977-78   Vice-President

1976-77   Finance Committee

1976   Treasurer

1975-80   Community Planning and Steering Committee

1973-80   Budget and Allocation Committee

1971-78   Board of Directors/Executive Committee

Womens' Conference Leadership:

1974   Board of Directors Women's Conference, Greater L.A.

1969   President-Women's Conference, San Fernando Valley

National Women's Division: United Jewish Appeal

1993   Women's Division Committee Member-Long
           Range Planning

1993   Women's Division Co-Chair - King David Society
           Event-Palm Springs

1993   Western Region Women's Division Chair – Endowments

1992   West Coast Co-Chair, UJA National Women's Division
           $25,000 event held in Los Angeles

1990-91   Co-Chair-National Women's Division(Israel Missions)

1989   Co-Chair-Western Region Women's Division Ruby
           Event, Santa Fe,New Mexico

1980   Co-Chair-$10,000 Women's Event,Los Angeles

1978   Chairman-Palm Springs National Women's
           Division$5,000 luncheon

1977-   National Board-Women's Division/UJA(Portfolio)

Community Consultant:

Speaker and Guest Speaker at fundraising events, helping and
inspiring success of fundraising campaigns and leadership for the
following communities: Palm Springs, Long Beach, Orange
County, Santa Barbara, Portland and Seattle.

JEWISH COMMUNITY FOUNDATION

1992-3   Vice President

1991   Chairman - Womens Committee of the JCF

1991   Board Member

1991   Vice President

1991   Executive Committee Member

JEWISH COMMUNITY CENTERS ASSOCIATION OF GREATER L.A.

1993   Discovery Museum Board Member

UNIVERSITY OF JUDAISM

1990   Chairman – Joel Grey Concert at the Gindi

1984-93 Co-Chair – Council on Continuing Education

1982   Leonard and Annette Shapiro were honored by the Patrons Society of the University which is an affiliate of the Jewish Theological Seminary in America. For many years, both have served on numerous committees and continue to be involved

HOMESAFE:

1979-85 Member of Advisory Committee. Homesafe is a child day care and foster home service which is part of the many programs at Vista Del Mar Child Care Center.

HEBREW UNION COLLEGE:

1978-83 Member of Committee for Jewish Communal Service

HADASSAH:

1953-54 President, Jr. Matron's Chapter (Supporting Hadassah Hospital in Israel)

UNITED WAY:

1967-71 In San Fernando Valley and Los Angeles:
         Special Gifts Campaign Western Region IV
         Board Member Western Region V
         Corporate Board Member-Greater Los Angeles
         Chairman-Child Care Allocation Committee

Member-Special Committee on Relationship with Health agencies in the community regarding new partners with United Way (i.e. ADA-Southern California Affiliate as new partner).

CULTURAL INVOLVEMENT:

Founders – Los Angeles Music Center

1988-   Blue Ribbon Committee

Founders – Museum of Contemporary Art (MOCA)

1991-92   Co-Chair/Products/Projects Council
1991   Co-Chair/Gala/Projects Council

PERSONAL:

Annette currently lives with her husband Leonard in Beverly Hills. They have three children and seven grandchildren

September, 1993

RECOGNITION & REWARDS

1956   KEY AWARD – For outstanding leadership and distinguished service on behalf of the Jewish Community, United Jewish Welfare Fund, Jr. Matrons-Valley Co-Chairman, Women's Division.

1963   PRESIDENTIAL AWARD – to Leonard and Annette Shapiro "for many years of Leadership and Devotion on behalf of the Jr. Sportsmen for the City of Hope."

1977   COUNTY OF LOS ANGELES COMMENDATION – "on her abilities, dedication and accomplishments; she is extended most sincere congratulations and best wishes for her continued success as one of Los Angeles County's most devoted volunteers." – Edmund D. Edelman, Supervisor, 3rd District.

1977   CITY OF BEVERLY HILLS – June 25 – "Annette Shapiro Day" for "outstanding contribution to her community for her devotion to the humanitarian ideals and objectives of the City of Hope."

1977   CITY OF LOS ANGELES – MAYOR'S CERTIFICATE OF APPRECIATION "to recognize the outstanding activities of Annette Shapiro" stating "Your community spirit and interest have helped make our City a better place in which to live..." – Tom Bradley, Mayor.

1982   CITY OF LOS ANGELES, State of California – to Annette and Leonard Shapiro, who, "have been chosen to receive THE ETERNAL LIGHT AWARD OF THE PATRONS SOCIETY of the University of Judaism.

1982   COUNTY OF LOS ANGELES – to Annette and Leonard Shapiro by the Board of Supervisors of the County of Los Angeles, that Annette and Leonard Shapiro "are hereby highly commended and warmly congratulated on their outstanding dedication, contributions and accomplishments on behalf of the Jewish Community."

1986   THE ADDISON B. SCOVILLE AWARD – for "outstanding contributions to The American Diabetes Association."

1987   THE "ANNETTE SHAPIRO AWARD" was established by the American Diabetes Association to honor a volunteer each year for their outstanding leadership and dedication, as demonstrated by Annette.

1988   GOLDA MEIR AWARD – "For outstanding community leadership." Jewish Federation Council of Greater Los Angeles – Women's Conference.

(Note: In light of the many awards and recognition received by Annette Shapiro, we have chosen to list just the few above as examples.)